Cambridge Regional G

Editors Harry Tolley, *School of Edu*
Keith Orrell, *Department of E*

The West Midlands

Brian Ellis
Department of Science Education, University of Warwick

The right of the
University of Cambridge
to print and sell
all manner of books
was granted by
Henry VIII in 1534.
The University has printed
and published continuously
since 1584.

Cambridge University Press

Cambridge
London   New York   New Rochelle
Melbourne   Sydney

Published by the Press Syndicate of the University of Cambridge
The Pitt Building, Trumpington Street, Cambridge CB2 1RP
32 East 57th Street, New York, NY 10022, USA
10 Stamford Road, Oakleigh Melbourne 3166, Australia

First published 1987

Printed in Great Britain by
The University Press, Cambridge

British Library Cataloguing in Publication Data
Ellis, Brian
The West Midlands.—(Cambridge regional geography)
1. Anthropo-geography——England——West Midlands
I. Title
304.2'09424'9   GF552.W4/
ISBN 0–521–27275–0

Acknowledgements

The publishers would like to thank the following for permission to reproduce illustrations: Aerofilms, figs. 1.3(a), 2.4, 2.5, 2.8, 2.9, 6.14, 7.2, 8.10; Annual Abstract of Statistics (CSO), Table 16; the author, figs. 1.3(b), 3.2, 3.3, 3.4, 3.12, 5.9, 5.13, 5.14, 6.1, 6.9, 6.10, 7.9, 8.1, 8.13; Berrow's Newspapers Limited, Worcester, fig. 1.5; British Tourist Authority, fig. 1.1; City of Birmingham Education Committee, fig. 6.7(b); City of Birmingham Environmental Health Department, fig. 6.11: County Council of Hereford and Worcester, Table 27; Coventry Evening Telegraph, fig. 5.9; Department of Employment, Table 13, Table 25; Department of Science Education, University of Warwick, fig. 2.12; Field Studies 5 (1980), *from* Job and Jarman, *Central Place Provision in Theory and Practice*, pp. 259–288, fig. 7.3, Table 25, Table 26; Geographical Magazine, September 1978, fig. 5.11; Geographical Magazine, October 1973, fig. 8.12; Geography vol 57, 1972, *from* M. J. Wise, *The Birmingham–Black Country Conurbation in Regional Geography*, fig. 7.7; HMSO, Table 3, figs. 6.7(a), 8.3(b); Macmillan, *from* Richardson, *Twentieth Century Coventry*, fig. 5.7; Ministry of Agriculture, Fisheries and Food, fig. 8.6(a), Table 29; A. Moyes, *Geography*, April 1974, fig. 3.9 (updated); National Coal Board, figs. 3.7, 3.8, 3.13, 3.14, Table 5, Table 6; National Union of Mineworkers, *The Miner*, July/August 1982, fig. 3.10; Ordnance Survey, fig. 8.9; Oxford University Press, *from* Gold, *Introduction to Behavioural Geography*, fig. 1.4; Pergamon, *from* Dennis and Clout, *A Social Geography of England and Wales*, fig. 5.7; Redditch Development Corporation, fig. 6.13; Rover Group plc, figs. 5.3(a) and (b); Staffordshire County Council, fig. 1.6; Tamworth District Council, Staffordshire, figs. 7.8(a) and (b); Warwickshire County Council Planning Department, fig. 3.5; Terry Weir, fig. 4.1; West Midlands County Council, Table 14; WMCC Stats 80, Table 12.

The author would like to thank Judy Parker for processing his photographs.

WV

Contents

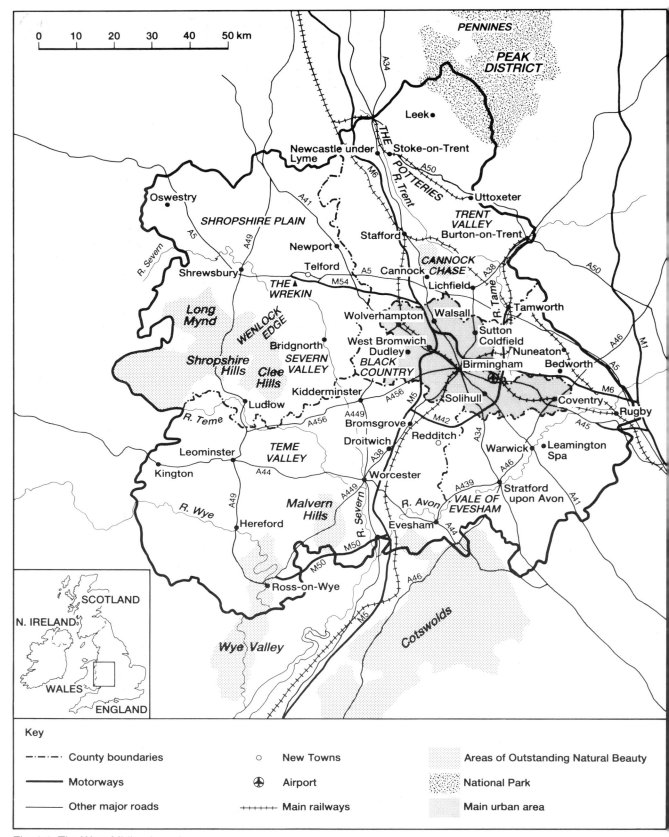

Fig. 1.1. The West Midlands region.

1 Images of the West Midlands

Fig. 1.2. 'Yes, but how will I know when I get there?'

---

image

Normally, 'image' means the outward appearance of something. In geography the word means not only what a place looks like but also includes our feelings about the place. You will have images of places you have never been to or even seen because of what you have read or heard about them. Geographers often call this developing a 'sense of place'.

Fig. 1.3. Urban landscapes: (a) a scene in Birmingham; (b) land reclamation at a derelict marl hole near Stoke-on-Trent, in the Potteries.

Pictures in the mind

Here you are starting to read a book on the West Midlands. What do you know already about the region? Does it bring any **images** to mind?

Write down a list of any things and places you associate with the West Midlands. You could do a survey among other people in the school and your family and friends outside school. Ask them to tell you the first three words or phrases that come into their minds when you say 'the West Midlands' to them. Make a note of their answers. When you have asked twenty or so people, work out the most common answers. What sort of picture do they have? How does it compare with yours?

Even if you do not live there or have never been there, you will probably have got some ideas about the West Midlands from newspapers, TV or radio. The following is an account of how one newcomer to the area feels about part of the West Midlands.

'When I left Canada everyone thought I was mad. "Why go to Birmingham?" they all said. "Birmingham is absolutely the end of the world!" But shortly before leaving, a woman who had emigrated from Birmingham said to me, comfortingly, "Don't worry. It's not true. Birmingham isn't the end of the world, but Wolverhampton, out in the Black Country – now that *is* the end of the world!"

Birmingham was a great shock. The city centre was so crowded. It was so dirty; there were no green spaces in the town. Having been told that Wolverhampton was the end of the world, I had to see it. On my first train trip there, I felt a wave of horrible depression at the sight of all the industrial wasteland. How could anyone live a happy, normal life in such surroundings?

But my perspective did change and I am now at home here. Several friends from Canada have been to visit me. We take day trips to Coventry, Stratford and Warwick; and then comes the hard stuff. It's out to the Black Country for Real Ale.'

Look at fig 1.3 and make a list of all the things on the photographs that could contribute to the poor image. Do you think the people who live in those houses think they are living at the 'end of the world'?

Good and bad images

Two areas of the West Midlands have such strong characteristics that they are known by names which reflect their images. One of these areas is the Black Country, referred to above. It was described by a geographer in 1902 like this:

'The whole district is one great workshop above ground and below. At night it is lurid with the flames of the iron furnaces; by day it appears one vast, loosely-knit town of humble homes amid cinder heaps and fields stripped of vegetation by smoke and fumes.'

Although the coal mines and iron furnaces are now closed and much of the pollution and derelict land has gone, the area is still called the Black Country. It has not been able to rid itself of its old image.

Fig. 1.4. Attractive and unattractive areas in Great Britain. When the research was done to produce this figure, it was discovered that wherever else people might like to live, they nearly always liked their home area. Why do you think this is? (We call this *place preference*, or *place loyalty*.) What do you like about the area where you live? What would you miss most if you went to live somewhere else? If you had plenty of money, where would you like to live?

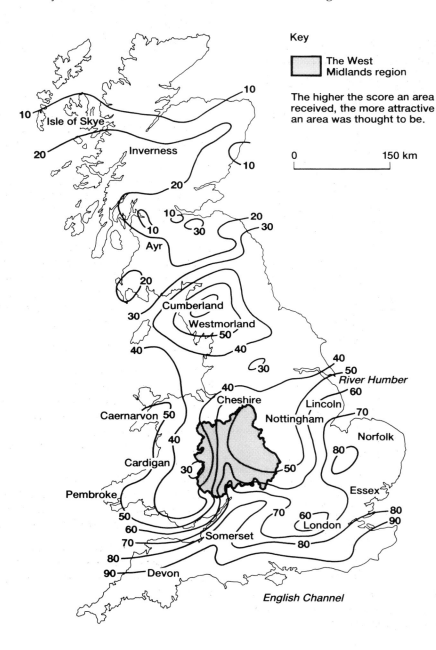

Key

The West Midlands region

The higher the score an area received, the more attractive an area was thought to be.

0   150 km

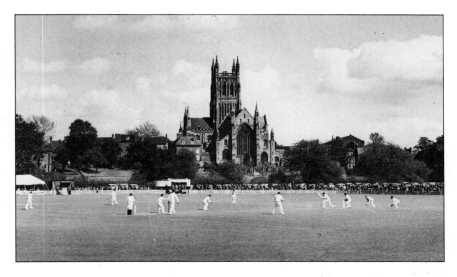

Fig. 1.5. Worcester Cathedral. The Midlands are sometimes called 'The Heart of England'. This 'typically English' scene is at Worcester County Cricket Ground, looking towards the imposing Worcester Cathedral, which is on a terrace of higher land overlooking the River Avon.

Staffordshire. A county of contrasts.

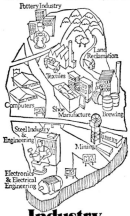

Industry.

Tourism.

Fig. 1.6. An advertisement produced recently by the Staffordshire County Planning Department.

The other area which has taken on a special name is the Potteries. This area, in and around Stoke-on-Trent, has the greatest concentration of china- and pottery-making in Britain and so the name 'the Potteries' is still appropriate. Like the Black Country, the Potteries had a dirty image. This is how one writer described it in 1933:

'Although there was more smoke than I had ever seen before, there were no tall chimneys, no factory buildings frowning over the street but only a fantastic collection of narrow-necked jars or bottles peeping above the house tops . . . But without those great bottles of heat there would be no Potteries. They represent the very heart and soul of the district.'   (J. B. Priestley, 1934)

Gas and electricity are now used to fire the kilns instead of coal, so the smoke problem has gone. Almost all the bottle-kilns have been demolished and the new factories are less distinctive.

Some parts of Britain are regarded as more attractive to live in than others. Fig. 1.4 shows the results of a survey of how attractive different parts of Britain were thought to be by school and university students.

How well did different parts of the West Midlands do in the survey?

Perhaps there are two faces to the West Midlands. There are the industrial towns that have poor images, while the rural areas (see fig. 1.5) are thought more attractive. Maybe if you were born and brought up in a West Midlands town you would not agree with that. Most people remain very loyal to their own home area.

It is now quite common to try and change the image of an area in order to 'sell' it to outsiders. A recent advertising campaign by one West Midlands county, Staffordshire, emphasised the differences between its traditional urban, industrial image and the attractions of its countryside. As you can see from the advertisement (fig. 1.6), it is even using the remains of its industrial past as one of its attractions.

What other sorts of image is it trying to create? Do you know of any examples of trying to create a new image for the area where you live? What would you write about your own area if you were running an advertising campaign to attract people to the area?

7

West Midlands on the map

This book is about the Standard Region of the West Midlands. That is the area shown on the map in fig. 1.7. The Standard Region is made up of the counties of Hereford and Worcester, Shropshire, Staffordshire, Warwickshire and the West Midlands Metropolitan County. Each of the counties is divided into districts and in the Metropolitan County these districts are called Metropolitan Districts. The old Metropolitan County is different from the others. It is made up almost entirely of towns and cities. Even this attempt to define the region is not without one source of confusion. We still have the words 'West Midlands' used for two different things: the West Midlands Standard Region, and the West Midlands Metropolitan County. However, the abolition of the Metropolitan Counties in 1986 eases this confusion.

Fig. 1.7. The West Midlands Standard Region.

Key

The West Midlands and the rest of Britain

We have so far looked at the West Midlands alone. A quick way of making some comparisons with other regions is to look at statistics which summarise basic facts about them.

Look at fig. 1.8 first. How does the population of the West Midlands compare with the rest of Britain with regard to total population, its rate of growth and density?

We can compare the West Midlands with other regions with regard to industry and farming and see if it really does deserve its reputation for being mainly industrial.

Fig. 1.9. The number of people employed in manufacturing industries in the Standard Regions.
Which region has the most people employed in manufacturing?
Which regions have more people employed in manufacturing than the West Midlands?
How many more people are employed in manufacturing in the South East than in the West Midlands?
Which regions have less than half a million people employed in manufacturing?
Which region has the least number of people employed in manufacturing?

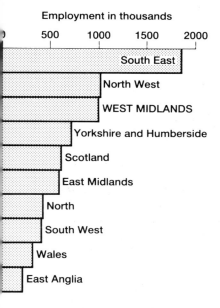

Employment in thousands

Fig. 1.8. Comparisons of the West Midlands and the other Standard Regions.

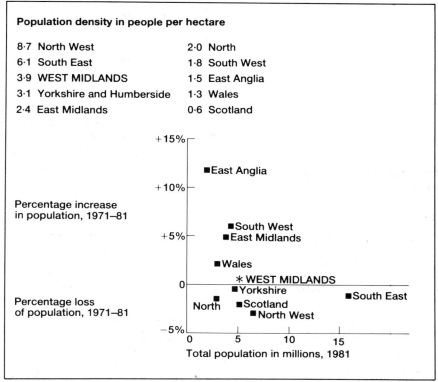

Population density in people per hectare

8·7 North West	2·0 North
6·1 South East	1·8 South West
3·9 WEST MIDLANDS	1·5 East Anglia
3·1 Yorkshire and Humberside	1·3 Wales
2·4 East Midlands	0·6 Scotland

Table 1 *The percentage of people employed in manufacturing industries in the Standard Regions.*

Rank order	Percentage of region's employees who work in manufacturing industries
1 WEST MIDLANDS	39.4
2 East Midlands	36.3
3 North West	32.6
4 Yorkshire and Humberside	30.4
5 North	30.3
6 East Anglia	27.3
7 South West	25.6
8 Wales	25.3
9 Scotland	25.2
10 South East	23.2

Before we look at the actual position, let's see what images you and the class have. In fig. 1.8 you have a list of the Standard Regions. Which ones do you think are mainly industrial and which mainly agricultural ones? Which region has most people employed in manufacturing? Compare your results with the rest of the class. Now let's compare your images with the reality.

Fig. 1.9 and Table 1 show two different ways of measuring the importance of industry. The bar chart (fig. 1.9) shows the actual numbers of people employed in manufacturing. However, the figures shown in fig. 1.9 do not give you the whole picture. One of the reasons the South East has so many people employed in manufacturing industry is that it has more people living there than any other region. So we also need to know what proportion of the people living in each region works in manufacturing industry. This is shown in Table 1.

Were you surprised by the facts when you compared them with your images of the regions?

Use the statistics in Table 1 and the map of the Standard Regions (fig. 1.10) to produce a map which will emphasise the ways in which the West Midlands is different from other regions. What conclusions can you draw about the West Midlands? Is the industrial image a fair one?

However, does the importance of industry mean that there is little open countryside? Look at Table 2. These statistics tell you that 75.4% of the West Midlands is used for agriculture. That means that three-quarters of the region is open countryside. So much for the 'all built-up' image! But how important is agriculture compared with other regions?

9

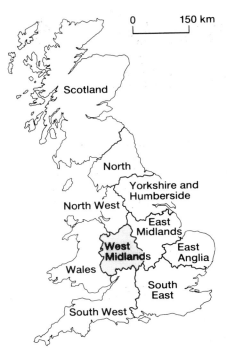

Fig. 1.10. A map of the Standard Regions.

The table gives you two different ways of measuring the importance of agriculture. What conclusions would you draw about the West Midlands?

Table 2 *Agriculture in the Standard Regions.*

	Percentage of the area of the region used for agriculture	Percentage of the workforce of the region employed in agriculture
East Anglia	80.6	6.3
East Midlands	79.5	2.2
North	68.7	1.3
North West	62.2	0.6
South East	63.7	1.1
South West	77.5	3.1
Wales	71.7	2.4
WEST MIDLANDS	75.4	1.4
Yorkshire and Humberside	71.6	1.6

Draw a bar chart similar to the one in fig. 1.9, arranging the regions so that the one with the greatest percentage is at the top and the one with the smallest percentage is at the bottom.
How does the West Midlands compare with other regions?

Looking at statistics in this way does tell us some things about the West Midlands and whether it deserves its image. However, there are more practical ways you might think about how the region compares with the rest of Britain. If you had the chance to live anywhere you wanted in Britain, you would want to know all sorts of things before you decided where to go. You would certainly be interested in average earnings, unemployment rate and the cost of houses, and that information for each region is given in Table 3.

Table 3 *Wages, unemployment and average house prices in the Standard Regions in the mid 1980s.*

	Average weekly earnings (£)		Unemployment rate in 1985 as percentage of total workforce	Average house prices at beginning of 1985 (£)
	Male	Female		
East Anglia	166	110	10.0	32,500
East Midlands	164	106	11.8	26,100
North	167	110	17.8	24,900
North West	171	112	15.6	25,900
Scotland	178	111	14.7	28,950
South East	198	130	9.4	41,450
South West	166	110	11.0	33,500
Wales	165	111	15.8	26,600
WEST MIDLANDS	167	110	15.0	28,200
Yorkshire and Humberside	167	107	14.0	23,400

Use this information to draw up a list of advantages and disadvantages of the West Midlands compared with other regions.

2 Landscapes of the West Midlands

If you look in an atlas at a relief map of Britain, you will see that most of the north and west is highland, but most of the south and east is lowland. The West Midlands region lies where the highlands and lowlands meet. Looking at fig. 2.1 it is very easy to think that these are distributed in a jumbled-up way, but there is a pattern to them. It might help you to sort the pattern out if you think about it in this way:

(a) The edges of the Welsh Mountains and the Pennines, which are parts of highland Britain, just reach into the West Midlands.

Fig. 2.1. The relief features of the West Midlands.

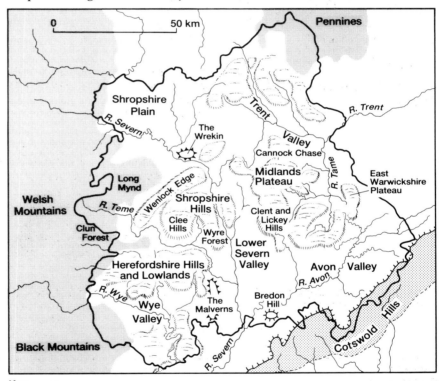

Key

HIGHLANDS

The highest land in the West Midlands; large areas are more than 300 metres above sea level

Isolated hill rising to over 300 metres

LOWLANDS

The lowest land in the West Midlands; it lies below 120 metres

HILL AREAS

Hilly areas where the land lies between 120 and 300 metres

A long ridge of higher land, which reaches nearly 250 metres above sea level. The ridge is called an escarpment and has a steep slope (the *scarp slope*) facing north-west and a more gentle slope (the *dip slope*) facing south-east

(b) Much of the landscape of the region is made up of a mixture of hills and plateaus. These fall into a series of groups:
  (i) the Shropshire Hills including Wenlock Edge, Clee Hills and Wyre Forest;
  (ii) the Midlands Plateau including Cannock Chase, the Clent and Lickey Hills and the East Warwickshire Plateau;
  (iii) the Herefordshire Hills.
(c) There are two main lowland areas:
  (i) the Shropshire Plain and the valley of the River Trent, which lie to the north of the hills;
  (ii) the Lower Severn Valley and the Avon Valley, which lie to the south of the hills.
(d) South-east of the Avon Valley, the edge of the West Midlands is formed by the long ridge of the Cotswold **escarpment.**

escarpment
A particular sort of hill, which is usually a long ridge with a steep scarp slope on one side and a more gentle dip slope on the other. An escarpment follows the outcrop of a gently dipping bed of rock (see fig. 2.1).

Geographers are interested in why the mountains, hills and lowlands are found where they are. Why do you find mountains in one place and lowlands somewhere else? The skeleton around which physical landscapes are developed is the geology. Rocks form the basis of the landscape in the same way that the bones of the skeleton make up the framework of the body. The appearance of the landscape depends on how the rocks are shaped and moulded by weathering, erosion and deposition. If a rock is hard it will be much more resistant to weathering and erosion than a soft one. So areas made of hard rocks are more likely to be mountainous or hilly. Areas of soft rock are more likely to be lowland.

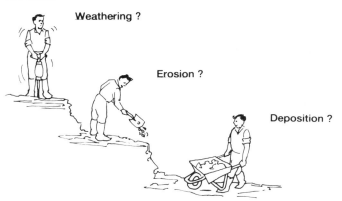

Fig. 2.2. Check that you really know what weathering, erosion and deposition mean!

hypothesis
Geographers use a general statement called a hypothesis when they have a hunch about how two sets of facts are related. The hunch is often written like this: 'We think that when one thing occurs it will cause something else to occur'; or 'If one thing is true then something else will also be true'. When geographers state a hypothesis they then usually set out to test if it works.

Let's test how well the **hypothesis** about the relationship between relief and geology works. Copy out the list of relief features (a)–(d) above into your notebook, and using figs. 2.1 and 2.3 say for each of the features if it is made of hard or soft rocks.
How well does the hypothesis 'the older the rocks the higher the land' work?
Are there any exceptions to the rule?
Why are old rocks usually harder and more resistant than newer ones?

If you have completed the list accurately it should support the hypothesis and show you that the high areas in the western part of the region are also the areas where the rocks are older than the Coal Measures. The lowest areas are found where the rocks are younger than the Coal Measures. The hill areas of the Midlands Plateau and the East Warwickshire Plateau are made mainly from Coal Measure rocks, which stick up, as islands, through the younger Permian and Triassic rocks of the lowlands.

Fig. 2.3. The geology of the West Midlands.

A |——|B   Line of cross section in Fig. 2.6

———   Boundary of West Midlands region

Note: This map covers exactly the same area as Fig. 2.1, The relief features of the West Midlands

0   50 km

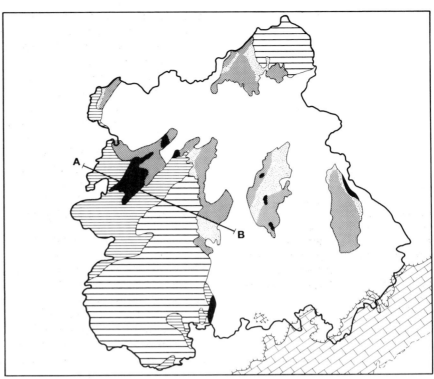

Geological Time Scale		Types of rock
Present day		
	Tertiary	There are no rocks as young as this in the West Midlands.
100 million years ago	Cretaceous	
	Jurassic	These are newer sedimentary rocks. They have had little compression and no baking because they have not been folded to make mountains. They are relatively soft rocks. Because they are soft they are easily weathered and eroded and form the low land in the West Midlands. Some beds of harder rocks form hills.
200 million years ago	Triassic	
	Permian	
300 million years ago	←— Rocks where workable coal is found } Coal Measures	These are old sedimentary rocks. They have been compressed but have not been hardened by baking. They are still hard enough to form the hill and plateau areas of the West Midlands.
400 million years ago	Lower Carboniferous and Devonian	
	Silurian	
	Ordovician	
500 million years ago	Cambrian	These rocks are very old. They have been compressed and baked very hard several times as they were being folded and raised up to become mountains. Because they are very hard they resist weathering and erosion and form the areas of highest land in the West Midlands. Metamorphic, igneous and sedimentary rocks are all found.
600 million years ago	Pre-Cambrian	

A mountain edge landscape

The photograph in fig. 2.4 is a good example of the upland landscapes in the western part of the West Midlands which have developed on old, hard rocks. The photograph was taken from an aircraft flying over the hill called Caer Caradoc. Some of the features on the photograph also appear on the cross section in fig 2.6.

Fig. 2.4. Aerial photograph of part of the upland landscape in the West Midlands.

Can you locate on the section where the photograph was taken from?
In which direction was the camera pointing?
If you wanted to collect examples of a volcanic rock and a metamorphic rock, which places on the photograph would you visit?

Now we can explain how some of the details of the landscape have been produced by erosion.

Look carefully at the Long Mynd Plateau on fig. 2.4: can you identify the following features in that area?
1. The high, flat plateau top with no valleys.
2. The eastern edge of the plateau falling steeply to the Church Stretton Valley.
3. Short river valleys with V-shaped **cross profiles** and steep zig-zag courses, cut into the edge of the plateau.

This landscape presents a problem for the geographer to explain. We know that the plateau is made up of hard, resistant rocks, but there are deep river valleys, like the Cardingmill, cutting into the edge of the plateau. These valleys suggest that the hard rocks are being worn away very successfully by rivers. The flow diagram in fig. 2.7 helps explain why the rivers here have enough power to erode the hard rocks.

---

cross profiles
Cross sections of the valley as you would see them if you were standing in the river and were looking along the valley. When they are drawn in diagrams they represent a slice across the valley at right-angles to the river or stream.

Fig. 2.5. Cross profiles.

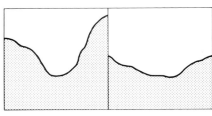

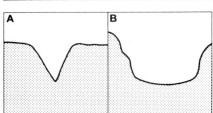

In the examples A and B above, which is the cross profile of the Cardingmill Valley and which the Church Stretton Valley (fig. 2.4)?

14

Fig. 2.6. Geological section across landscapes formed on old, hard rocks.

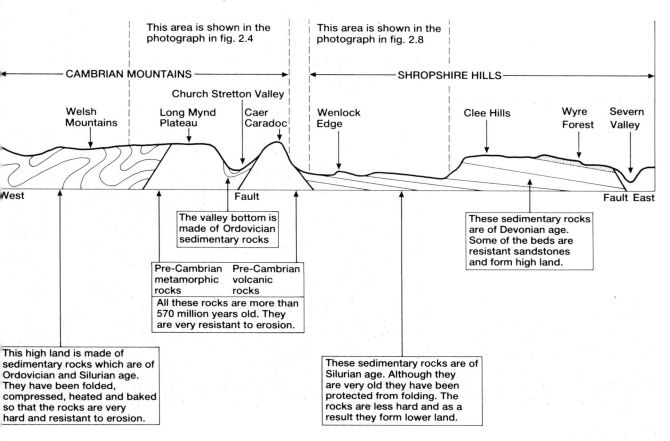

Fig. 2.7. Flow diagram to explain how the edge of the Long Mynd Plateau is being eroded.

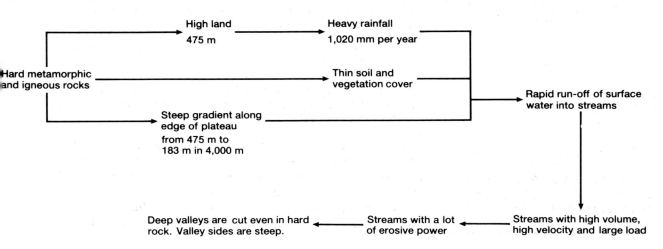

An escarpment landscape

Fig. 2.8 is a photograph of another type of landscape made up of old rocks. The area is made of rocks which are of Silurian age and it lies to the east of Caer Caradoc. You can see from the cross section in fig. 2.6 that the land is much lower than on the Long Mynd and Caer Caradoc. There is an explanation on the diagram of why it is lower, despite the fact that the rocks are old. The landscape is not all the same height. There are two lines of hills called **escarpments** running away into the distance. On each side of the escarpments are broad, shallow, gently rolling valleys. These are usually called clay vales. Escarpments and clay vales are further examples of how rock hardness affects landscapes. These landscapes form where alternating beds of hard and soft rocks dip gently underground. Because the hard rocks are more resistant to erosion, they form the escarpments. Where the edge of the rock bed meets the surface, the steep scarp slope is formed. The more gentle dip slope is formed where the rock bed dips underground. The soft rocks are less resistant to erosion and they underlie the river valleys between the escarpments.

Look again at the photograph and diagram in fig. 2.8.
Which are the hard rocks which form the escarpments?
Which are the soft rocks which form Ape Dale and Hope Dale?
Why do you think the river valleys between escarpments are called clay vales?

Fig. 2.8. Escarpment landscape at Wenlock Edge in the Shropshire Hills.

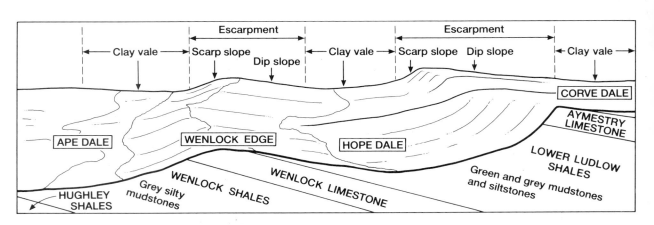

Lowland landscapes

The Shropshire Plain

The photograph (fig. 2.9) is of part of the Shropshire Plain, which is one of the largest lowlands in the West Midlands. This is a very different landscape from the ones we have studied already.

g. 2.9. The Shropshire Plain.

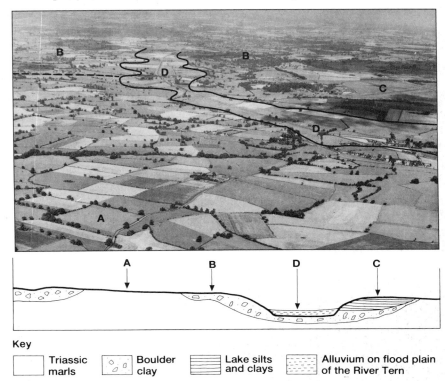

Key

☐ Triassic marls	Boulder clay	Lake silts and clays	Alluvium on flood plain of the River Tern

Can you predict whether it will be made of relatively old or young rocks? Will they be hard or soft? Look at figs. 2.1 and 2.3 and check if you were right.

Like most of the lowlands of the West Midlands the Shropshire Plain is made of Permian and Triassic rocks. The rocks in the area A on the photograph are marls (a very stiff clay-like rock), which erode very easily. So one reason for the landscape being low and flat is the soft rock. But that does not explain all the landscape features. Many of these are the result of the area having a different climate in the past. For most of the last half-million years Britain had a much colder climate than now. During this period – the Ice Age – glaciers from Wales, the Pennines and the Irish Sea flowed over the Shropshire Plain into the West Midlands.

The ground-up rock carried by the ice now forms patches of glacial deposits which cover the solid rocks. For example, on the photograph at B there are **boulder clays** from the bed of the glaciers and **outwash sands and gravels** from meltwater streams. At C there are silts and clays which were laid down in small lakes. If you dug a trench through these deposits you could see how they are related to each other. You could then draw a diagram like the cross section in fig. 2.9.

Work out from that section which are the youngest and oldest glacial deposits. Is the alluvium in the flood plain of the River Tern (D on the photograph) older or younger than the glacial deposits?

Boulder clay and **outwash sands and gravels**

Thin surface layers of rock which were formed during the Ice Age (i.e. in the last half-million years).

Boulder clay: Irregular, broken-up pieces of rock mixed with clay. It is produced by rock being ground up along the bed of a moving glacier. So if you find a patch of boulder clay, it shows that the area was once underneath a glacier.

Outwash sands and gravels: As water from melting ice runs out of a glacier it brings with it some of the ground-up rock from the ice. The running water wears the irregular rock fragments into pebbles, gravels and sands, and washes away the clay. Large quantities of the sands and gravels are left behind along the valley bottoms after all the ice has melted.

gorge

A river valley which is particularly deep, steep-sided and narrow. Gorges are usually found where rivers cut into areas of high land. Very often the river fills the whole of the valley bottom.

Fig. 2.10. A gorge.

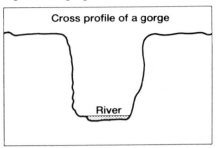

Cross profile of a gorge

River

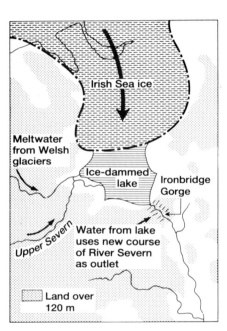

Fig. 2.11. Diversion of the River Severn.

Fig. 2.12. Glacial deposits in the Avon Valley. The light-coloured sediments in the bottom half of the quarry face are sands and gravels which were deposited in the glacial lake. The dark deposits at the top of the quarry are boulder clay.

One result of ice covering the Shropshire Plain is very much more spectacular. The ice made the River Severn change its course. Before the Ice Age the upper part of the River Severn was a tributary of the River Dee and flowed into the Irish Sea. During the Ice Age, glaciers covered the Shropshire Plain as far south as the Shropshire Hills. Meltwaters from the ice could only escape by flowing southwards between the ice and the hills. In doing this the water cut a deep **gorge** through the watershed. Near the end of the Ice Age, when the glaciers began to melt and retreat, the water formed a large lake, which rose until it reached the gorge cut earlier and flowed away through it to join the Lower Severn (fig 2.11).

After the Ice Age, when the glaciers had completely disappeared, the new gorge was lower than the old course of the Upper Severn, which was partly blocked and made higher by glacial deposits. So the Upper Severn joined the Lower Severn via the Ironbridge Gorge to take its present route to the Bristol Channel.

The Avon Valley

The landscape of the Avon Valley, which is the lowland in the south-east of the region, was also affected by the Ice Age. A large glacier made a dam across the northern part of the valley, and meltwater streams which flowed out of the glaciers and across the bare land surface formed a lake. They carried large amounts of sediment which formed thick beds of sand and gravel in the lake (fig. 2.12).

The glaciers continued to grow and the ice advanced across the lake bed, covering the sand and gravel with boulder clay. When the glaciers melted at the end of the Ice Age, the River Avon and its tributaries began to cut into the glacial deposits. They are soft and easily eroded, so the rivers cut down through them very quickly. Most of the deposits were washed down to the sea. However, some were redeposited by the river as a series of terraces, which now cover most of the floor of the valley. The terrace deposits make very fertile soils and have helped the Avon Valley to become one of the richest farming areas in the West Midlands.

3 Using the rocks

Rocks are not only a major part of the landscape. They are also **resources** which may be exploited. Exploitation occurs when rocks which have commercial value are mined and quarried. The general name given to that industry is the **extractive industry**. We shall study two examples, the mining of coal and the quarrying of sand and gravel, to see what part they play in the geography of the West Midlands.

Wherever rocks are mined or quarried for raw materials, the production processes have some features in common. These features have led geographers to describe mineral extraction as a 'robber economy' or 'the destructive occupation of the land'. Look at the following list of features associated with mining and quarrying and see if you think the geographers' descriptions are good ones.

(a) Extraction eventually leads to the using up of the supplies of the raw material at that place, so mining and quarrying are always temporary industries. However, big mines and quarries might be worked for over a hundred years.
(b) Many rocks and minerals are **non-renewable** resources. This means that they are usually destroyed when they are used.
(c) At best they are difficult or expensive to **recycle**. So searches are always going on for new sources to replace the old ones.
(d) During mining and quarrying the environment is disturbed. In the case of quarrying the landscape is actually destroyed as the rocks are removed. Mineral extraction usually leads to a need for **land reclamation**.
(e) Because the products are bulky or heavy, special transport is needed and this too affects the environment of the area.
(f) The products of mining and quarrying are raw materials for other industries. These manufacturing industries may be attracted to the mining and quarrying areas, turning them into industrial regions.

In the rest of this chapter we will test how well these generalisations apply to sand and gravel quarrying and to coal mining in the West Midlands.

Quarrying sand and gravel

There are many sources of sand and gravel in the West Midlands. The pebble beds in the Permian and Triassic rocks (fig. 2.3) and the glacial and river deposits (figs. 2.9 and 2.12) are particularly useful. One area of production is the Tame Valley between Birmingham and Coventry (fig. 3.1).

Resources

Geographers use the word 'resources' for those things occurring naturally on the earth which we recognise as being useful as sources of wealth. They are usually specific things like:
- rock or mineral which can be mined or quarried (e.g. coal, limestone, gold, sand);
- soil in which we can grow food, or vegetation, such as grass which animals graze, or forest which can be used as a source for wood or paper;
- or water which can be collected into reservoirs to become a source of drinking water.

However, you can also think of beautiful landscape or scenery as a resource when it is used for recreation or holidays. A rock outcrop, a forest or a reservoir are all potential resources.

Extractive industry

In the West Midlands, the rocks which are used as resources by being mined or quarried are:
- clay – bricks, cement, earthenware, pottery
- coal – fire
- igneous – building stone, road chippings
- limestone – building stone, cement, road chippings
- sand and gravel – building sand, concrete
- sandstone – building stone, sand

Land reclamation

Using resources often leaves the land in such a mess that special steps have to be taken to clear up the mess and restore the land so that it can be used again. The process of improvement is called land reclamation. This is often expensive and is a hidden cost in the exploitation of the resources.

Fig. 3.1. Quarrying sand and gravel in the Tame Valley.

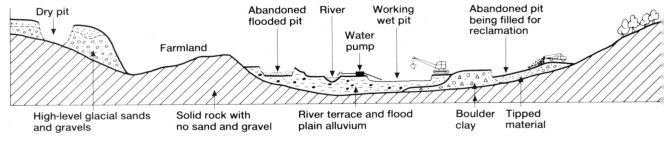

Key

River terrace and flood plain alluvium is a mixture of fine silt, sand and gravel which has to be washed and sorted before it can be used. The silt is no use in the building industry but it can be used for filling old pits.

Boulder clay has a lot of clay and boulders mixed with the sands and gravels and so has more waste which must be removed before the sands and gravels can be used. This waste is also used for filling old pits.

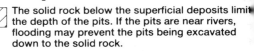
Glacial sands and gravels often contain fine sands which are used for making mortar and plaster, and coarse sands and gravels which are used for making concrete.

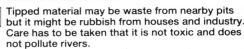
The solid rock below the superficial deposits limits the depth of the pits. If the pits are near rivers, flooding may prevent the pits being excavated down to the solid rock.

Tipped material may be waste from nearby pits but it might be rubbish from houses and industry. Care has to be taken that it is not toxic and does not pollute rivers.

non-renewable and renewable resources, recycling

A non-renewable resource is one which is destroyed when it is used. Most rocks and minerals are non-renewable: coal is burnt, concrete is not re-usable. It is possible to delay this destruction by re-using some metals when they become scrap. Re-using resources is often called recycling but it is often expensive or difficult.

Other resources are renewable. In some cases this occurs naturally. When water is used it is not destroyed but eventually finds its way back to the earth as rain. In other cases, we help in the renewal process by adding manure and fertiliser to soils or by sowing crops and replanting forests.

Working sand and gravel in the Tame Valley

The gravel workings are located along the floor and sides of the Tame Valley (fig. 3.1). When Warwickshire County Planning Department did an environmental survey, they said that the workings were one of the ugliest bits of landscape in the county. This is mainly because of the way in which the quarrying process destroys the landscape. The 'Minerals Plan for Warwickshire' describes how this destruction occurs:

'The material is removed by dragline. The topsoil is removed by scraper and is stored in banks which may be used as screens. The dug material is loaded either onto dump-trucks or onto a conveyor system to transfer it to a processing plant, consisting of machinery, conveyors and storage bins usually about 50 feet high and perhaps 300 or 400 feet long. There the material is crushed, washed and graded to produce clean sand and gravel, which is stored in stockpiles close to the plant. The product, where it is made into concrete on the site, leaves the quarry in mixer trucks, but otherwise is transported by lorries which carry 20 tons. A major pit will average some 40 vehicle movements per day. The working involves the upheaval of the surface of otherwise tranquil farmland and frequently the removal of hedgerows and their trees. Dry weather brings the risk of dust nuisance and wet weather the risk of mud on the highway.'

Fig. 3.2. Sand and gravel working in the Tame Valley, near Kingsbury. Read the description of sand and gravel working from the 'Minerals Plan for Warwickshire', and see how many of the things mentioned there you can identify on the photograph. Draw a sketch of the photograph in your notebook and label it to show these things.

Fig. 3.3. A concrete products factory near Kingsbury. This factory makes concrete blocks and pipes, which you can see being stored. This small manufacturing industry has been attracted to the area by the supplies of sand and gravel produced nearby. It uses very large amounts of these raw materials and so saves transport costs on them, but it still has to buy cement. The nearest supply is at Rugby, 40 kilometres away. Discuss in class the problems this factory will face when all the local sand and gravel has been used up.

Figs. 3.2 and 3.3 illustrate some of the ways in which the Tame Valley is affected by the industry. Remember, however, that in order to build houses, factories, shops and roads we need the building materials which are made with the sand and gravel. The planners have to try to reduce the impact of the quarries while they are operating.

Land reclamation, or clearing up the mess

Look at fig. 3.4. The lake used to be a gravel pit and once looked like the area in fig. 3.2. It has been reclaimed to form part of Kingsbury Water Park, opened in 1975 as a recreation area, situated between Birmingham and Coventry.

Fig. 3.5 is a map of the park. Examine the map and photographs carefully and work out what changes have taken place since quarrying finished.

Fig. 3.4. Bodymoor Heath Water, at Kingsbury Water Park. The land to the right of the lake has been made up by infilling with pulverised fly ash from the Hams Hall power stations, which you can see in the background.

The reclamation has been brought about in two ways. Some of the old water-filled pits were drained, their floors smoothed out and the banks made more regular and gentle. They were then re-filled with water, stocked with fish and the banks planted with trees. These pools are now used by fishermen. Other pits were cleaned up in similar ways and turned into lakes. You can see on the map how they are now used. Not all the old pits were restored in this way. Some have been filled in to create land for other uses. Fortunately, near Kingsbury there are two electric power stations, whose coal-fired boilers produce waste ash. This ash is pulverised (that means turned into powder) and is then used to fill the gravel pits. This reclaimed land is used in the park for the caravan

21

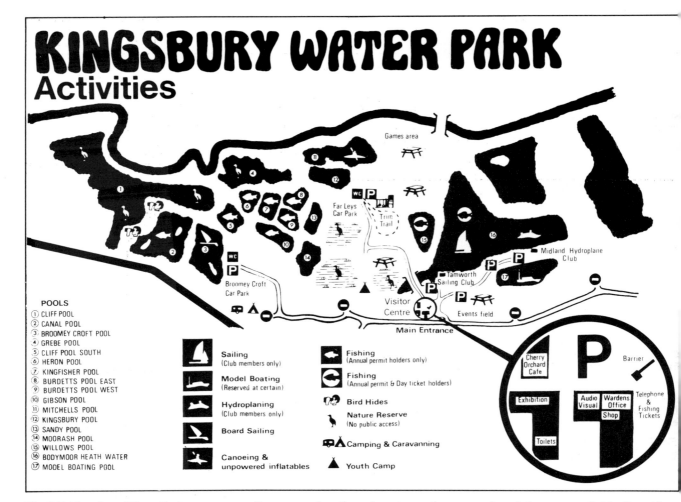

KINGSBURY WATER PARK
Activities

Games area

Far Leys Car Park

Trim Trail

Broomey Croft Car Park

Midland Hydroplane Club

Tamworth Sailing Club

Visitor Centre

Events field

Main Entrance

POOLS
1. CLIFF POOL
2. CANAL POOL
3. BROOMEY CROFT POOL
4. GREBE POOL
5. CLIFF POOL SOUTH
6. HERON POOL
7. KINGFISHER POOL
8. BURDETTS POOL EAST
9. BURDETTS POOL WEST
10. GIBSON POOL
11. MITCHELLS POOL
12. KINGSBURY POOL
13. SANDY POOL
14. MOORASH POOL
15. WILLOWS POOL
16. BODYMOOR HEATH WATER
17. MODEL BOATING POOL

Sailing (Club members only)

Model Boating (Reserved at certain)

Hydroplaning (Club members only)

Board Sailing

Canoeing & unpowered inflatables

Fishing (Annual permit holders only)

Fishing (Annual permit & Day ticket holders)

Bird Hides

Nature Reserve (No public access)

Camping & Caravanning

Youth Camp

Cherry Orchard Cafe

Barrier

Exhibition

Audio Visual | Wardens Office | Telephone & Fishing Tickets

Shop

Toilets

Fig. 3.5. Kingsbury Water Park activities.

What sorts of recreational activities are catered for at Kingsbury? Why have the planners tried to separate different sorts of activities into different areas? How have they tried to separate them? How well does the park seem to cater for parents with young children, naturalists, teenagers, elderly people? Does it look the sort of place you would like to go? Is it the sort of place people go to for a day or for a week? How do you think the fact that it is between Coventry and Birmingham affects the way it is used?

site, car parks, the adventure playground and the events field. Outside the park similar reclaimed land is used for farming.

Turning the old pits into recreational land is not the only use that has been found for them. The River Tame is one of the most polluted rivers in the country. It rises in the Black Country and flows through Birmingham before reaching the gravel working area. During its course through the built-up area it receives a lot of waste from industry and dirt and oil off the roads, which include the M6. The Severn-Trent Water Authority, which is responsible for the river, decided to create a lake out of a gravel pit and to use it to begin to clean the river. When the river flows into the lake it slows down and the grit and dirt being carried by the river sinks. The river flows out of the other end of the lake much cleaner. The polluted sediment is then dredged out of the lake and is taken away to be dumped in another abandoned quarry.

This study of sand and gravel working in the Tame Valley illustrates very well how we can set about changing the landscape in both destructive and constructive ways. It also shows how changes in one part of the landscape can affect other parts. The diagram in fig. 3.6 is a good way of showing how all these changes relate to each other. The old landscape is at the bottom of the diagram. If you start there you can follow pathways of change up through the diagram, until at the top you reach the landscape as it is now.

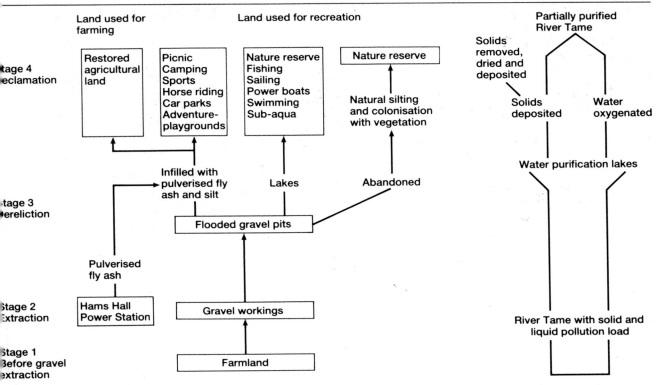

Fig. 3.6. A systems diagram showing the development of the land use pattern in the area affected by sand and gravel extraction in the Tame Valley.

Mining coal

Unlike sand and gravel, which is quarried from the surface, coal is usually mined from underground. These mines can be as much as 1,000 metres deep. The entrance to the mine is usually by a vertical shaft, over which stands the winding gear. This can be seen in fig. 3.7. The miners go to work down these shafts, the coal is brought up through them, all machinery for the mining has to go down them and they are also used for ventilating the mine. Underground the coal is found in layers or seams. In a mine 1,000 metres deep there may be only two or three seams worked and each will probably be only a metre or so thick. The coal is mined by following the seams and cutting the coal out in slices.

Fig. 3.7. Pithead gear at Daw Mill Colliery in Warwickshire. Space has to be found not only for the winding gear, but also for the coal washing and sorting plant, railway sidings, baths and canteen, offices and car parks.

23

Fig. 3.8. Coal-cutting machinery at Daw Mill Colliery. The revolving coal-cutting head is dragged along the coalface and takes out a slice of coal. Before it can take out the next slice, the conveyor which removes the coal and the roof supports (they prevent the roof collapsing onto the working space) is also moved forward. This is done by hydraulic jacks.

This is what is being done in fig. 3.8. When the coal has been cut it is taken by conveyor belt along underground roadways to the bottom of the shaft, where it is lifted to the surface in large skips.

The rocks that include seams of coal along with clays, sandstones and mudstones are called the Coal Measures. If you look back at fig. 2.3 on page 13 you will see that the Coal Measures are found in four places in the West Midlands. When coal is mined from these areas they are called coalfields.

The **exposed coalfields** are shown on fig. 3.9. The map shows that big changes have taken place in the mining industry, and there is more information about these changes in Table 4.

exposed and concealed coalfields
When a coalfield is developed where the Coal Measures outcrop (that is, they are exposed on the surface) it is usually called an exposed coalfield. Often the Coal Measures are covered over by other rocks and the coal can only be reached by drilling the mine through the other rocks down into the Coal Measures. Such a coalfield is called a concealed coalfield. As exposed coalfields gradually become exhausted, mining often extends into the concealed fields.

Table 4 *Coal production in the West Midlands.*

	1950	1970/71	1980/81	1983/84
Coal produced (million tonnes)				
West Midlands	17.7	11.3	9.2	7.3
Great Britain	205.5	135.4	109.6	89.5
Number of men employed (thousands)				
West Midlands	56.5	19.7	17.1	14.0
Great Britain	690.8	287.2	229.8	191.0
Coal produced per man in one year (tonnes)				
West Midlands	313	573	538	521
Great Britain	297	471	476	468

Make a list of what you think are the main changes.
Draw three line graphs to show the trends in the amount of coal produced, the number of men employed, and the amount produced per man in the West Midlands between 1950 and the 1980s.
Using the information in fig 3.9, draw another graph to show the number of mines working in 1950 and the 1980s.
What evidence can you get from fig 3.8 to help explain the changes in the amount of coal produced per man?

Fig. 3.9. Location of coal mines in the West Midlands in 1950 and the mid 1980s.
How many coalfields were working in 1950 and the 1980s, and what were their names? Draw up a table to show how many mines there were on each coalfield in 1950 and the mid 1980s. What was the total number of mines in 1950 and in the mid 1980s for the West Midlands? During that time, how many mines opened and how many closed?

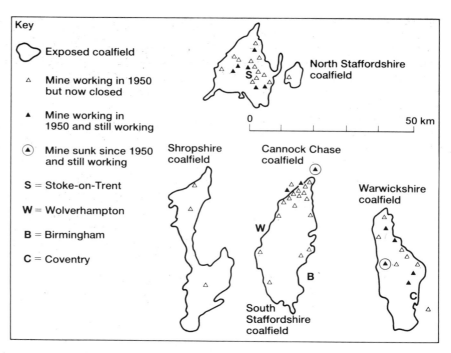

Employment and production, exhaustion and redundancies

Your list of the changes which have taken place in the West Midlands coal mining industry might have made you think of the following questions:
(a) Why have so many mines closed?
(b) What happens to the miners?
(c) What do the miners think about mines closing?
(d) What happens to the areas after the mines close?
As you can see from the extract (fig. 3.10) from a speech by Arthur Scargill, the President of the National Union of Mineworkers, the official policy of the Union is 'No pit closures unless from exhaustion'. There was a year-long strike about this between March 1984 and March 1985. However, you will remember from the beginning of this chapter that in

Fig. 3.10. A newspaper extract of part of a speech made by Arthur Scargill, President of the National Union of Mineworkers.

'If we do not save our pits from closure then all our other struggles become meaningless'

No pit closures unless from exhaustion, an investment programme to develop to the full the potential of existing collieries and a commitment from the Government and the NCB to sink "at least 30 new pits" – those were the policies for the expansion of the industry, stressed by NUM President Arthur Scargill in his first Presidential Address.

"The first priority for the Union," the new President emphasised, "is to protect the coal industry from the ravages of the market mechanism, the short-sightedness of politicians and deliberate political decisions designed to destroy our industry, jobs and communities. If we do not save our pits from closure, then all our struggles become meaningless!"

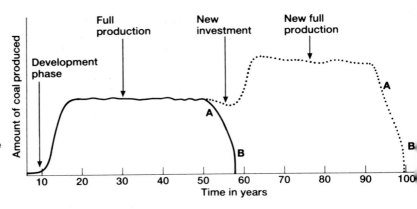

——— Normal life cycle of a mine

········ Extended life of a mine

A Accessible coal becoming exhausted. The costs of mining rise, productivity decreases and it becomes more difficult to make a profit.

B Coal is exhausted and mine has to close.

In some mines it is possible to invest money in improvement schemes in order to extend the life of the mine. But even when this happens, the time must eventually come when the mine will become unprofitable and then exhausted and will have to close.

Fig. 3.11. The life cycle of a coal mine.

any extractive industry, the minerals will eventually be used up and the mine or quarry must then close down. Some of the mine closures in the West Midlands have been for this reason. But there are other causes.

(a) Coal mines no longer making a profit.

If you look at fig. 3.11 you can see that every coal mine must reach a point in its life where the cost of running the mine becomes greater than the income earned by selling the coal. In 1950 most mines in the West Midlands were about fifty years old. In some cases it was possible to modernise them (see Table 5) but many closed.

Table 5 *Coal mines in the West Midlands in the early 1980s.*

	Date of first shaft	Production (million tonnes)	Number of men employed	Output per man (tonnes per year)
North Staffordshire coalfield				
Florence	1874 I	0.83	1,423	585
Hem Heath	1924 I	1.17	1,821	640
Holditch	1912	0.25	674	370
Silverdale	1880 I	0.52	845	615
Victoria	1850	0.23	607	380
Wolstanton	1918 I	0.51	1,273	400
Cannock Chase coalfield				
Lea Hall	1954 P	1.30	2,320	560
Littleton	1899 I	0.85	2,000	425
West Cannock	1914 I	0.42	818	515
Warwickshire coalfield				
Baddesley	1850 I	0.55	1,050	525
Birch Coppice	1875 I	0.50	1,030	485
Coventry	1912 P	0.70	1,300	540
Daw Mill	1958 P	1.10	1,250	880
Newdigate	1898 C	0.26	770	340

I = Major underground improvement scheme undertaken.
P = Major underground improvement scheme planned or in progress.
C = Pit closed in 1982.

Draw a column graph to show how many mines opened between 1850 and 1874, 1875 and 1899, 1900 and 1924, 1925 and 1949, 1950 and 1975.
What does this graph tell you about the age of most of the working mines? If you compare the ages of the mines with the diagram of the life cycle of of a coal mine (fig. 3.11), can you explain why most mines have had improvement schemes carried out?

If you had to predict which mines in the West Midlands are most at risk of closing, which mines would you choose and why would you choose them?

If a mine is costing more to run than it is earning from selling its coal, but still has coal which could be mined, the National Union of Mineworkers would try to prevent it being closed. Would you agree with keeping these mines open or would you favour closing them? (This is a good topic for a class discussion.)

(b) A fall in the demand for coal.

In 1950 about 200 million tonnes of coal were used in Britain but by 1980 this had fallen to about 110 million tonnes. An important reason for this decline was that the market for coal had changed. In 1950 most houses were heated by coal fires, steam trains ran on the railways, gas was produced from coal for use in the home and in industry, and much of the fuel used in industry was coal. Table 6 tells you what the present position is.

Table 6 *The markets for coal from the West Midlands coalfields.*

	Cannock Chase (%)	North Staffordshire (%)	Warwickshire (%)	Great Britain (%)
Power stations	84.7	77.6	56.4	70.4
Coke ovens	–	11.3	–	7.4
Industry	5.5	4.2	25.8	7.6
Domestic	9.7	7.0	17.7	4.8

What is the main use made of coal (see also fig. 3.12)?
What are the other markets?
Which coalfield is the most dependent on one market?
Which coalfield has the most varied markets?
What are the dangers of the coal industry depending on one market?

(c) Competition from other sources of energy.

If you look at Table 7 you can see that in 1950 coal was the dominant source of energy. But since then the position has changed dramatically.

Table 7 *Sources of energy consumed in Great Britain.*

	1950 (%)	1960 (%)	1970 (%)	1980 (%)	1983 (%)
Coal	94.5	82.6	46.7	35.9	35.0
Petroleum	4.9	16.6	44.7	37.9	34.8
Nuclear and HEP	0.6	0.8	3.2	4.3	6.0
Natural gas	–	–	5.3	21.7	24.0

Fig. 3.12. Lea Hall Colliery and Rugeley Power Stations. The two power stations on this site take their coal directly from Lea Hall Colliery, on the Cannock Chase coalfield, but they also have railway sidings for receiving coal from other collieries.
Can you identify the pithead gear of the coal mine, the cooling towers, the generator buildings and coal-loading equipment of the power stations?

Discuss with your neighbour or your teacher what is the best sort of diagram to draw, using the statistics in Table 7, to help you illustrate the changes in importance of different fuels in Great Britain.

What are these changes? It would be a good discussion topic for the class to explain how these changes have come about. Have you seen any adverts on TV or in newspapers and magazines which are trying to persuade people to go back to using coal (it's often called 'solid fuel' in the adverts)? For what sorts of uses can coal compete with oil, gas and electricity?

For a mixture of reasons there are now fewer, but larger and more productive, coal mines in the West Midlands (fig. 3.12).

27

Fig. 3.13. Drilling rigs like this one are used to search for new sources of coal. The drill takes out a 'core' of rock about 10 centimetres in diameter. These cores are brought to the surface and examined by geologists who can then work out the underground rock structure. They look for coal seams at least 1 metre thick, if the area is to be a worthwhile development as a coalfield.

Coal in the future

As existing coal mines and coalfields become worked out and coal production falls, British Coal has to search for new sources of supply. It usually does this by trying to see whether it is possible to follow existing coal seams on exposed coalfields into the surrounding areas. By working outwards from the exposed field, drilling boreholes (fig. 3.13) and making seismic surveys, British Coal has been able to follow the coal in the East Warwickshire field southwards. This could become the location of a new coalfield: the South Warwickshire coalfield. If British Coal decides that there is enough good-quality coal to mine and that it can be mined economically then there will be a Public Planning Inquiry to examine the plans and to consider any opposition.

An important part of the plans would be the decision on how many mines to sink and where to locate them. Some of the information that would be considered is given in fig. 3.14.

Imagine that you are responsible for planning the South Warwickshire coalfield. Where would you recommend British Coal to locate the mine? How many do you think it would be worth while sinking?

The way the planner would set about deciding this is to use a method called 'a Planning Sieve'. This usually involves eliminating all the areas that cannot be used and then choosing the best places in the areas that are left.
These are the stages you could go through to reach your decision:

1. Trace the map with the coal seams marked on it.
2. Lay it over the settlement map and mark on your traced map all the areas where you consider the mine could not be located. Reasons for this will include: too near another mine; seams too deep; seams too thin. What other reasons would there be?
3. This will leave you with lots of places where the mine(s) might be placed.
4. Now, again using the information on the maps and table, choose some specific sites where you could locate the mine and decide which of these you think is the best. To help you decide this you might want to think about how the mine will affect the area in which it is sunk, particularly as the changes will last a long time.

Now write a report for the Planning Inquiry giving your recommendations, including your maps and explaining the choices you have made.

As the area you have chosen is now almost certainly a country area with farms, villages and small towns, it is likely that many people would object to coal mining coming to the area. Here is a list of groups of people who might object. Copy it out and under each name list what you think their objections would be.

1. The farmers whose land would be taken.
2. Other farmers.
3. People who have lived in the villages all their lives.
4. People who have moved to live in the villages rather than live in Coventry.
5. People who live in nearby towns.
6. People interested in conservation of wildlife.

Can you add any more to the list? Can you think of any people who would support British Coal?

If you had the chance to give evidence to the planning inquiry, would you support or oppose the development of the coalfield? Sinking a mine here would change the geography of the area, but the geography of areas is always changing. Are the advantages of maintaining Britain's supply of coal and providing jobs for miners so big that it is worth spoiling part of rural Warwickshire? Or will the changes affect such a small area that it's not worth making a fuss about?

Fig. 3.14. Development of the South Warwickshire coalfield.

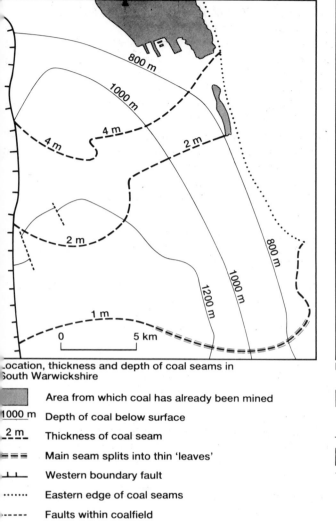

Location, thickness and depth of coal seams in South Warwickshire

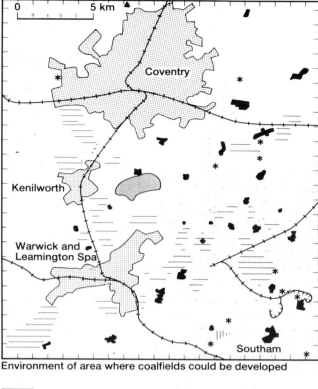

Environment of area where coalfields could be developed

▨	Area from which coal has already been mined
1000 m	Depth of coal below surface
2 m	Thickness of coal seam
≡≡≡	Main seam splits into thin 'leaves'
⊥⊥⊥	Western boundary fault
········	Eastern edge of coal seams
------	Faults within coalfield
▲	Coventry colliery

▨	Towns
✹	Villages
++++	Railways
▨	National Agricultural Centre and Royal Show ground
=	Grade 2 agricultural land (good quality)
|||	Grade 5 agricultural land (poor quality)
*	Nature Reserves and Sites of Special Scientific Interest
⌢⌢⌢	Limestone quarry

Factors affecting the possible location of a new coal mine in South Warwickshire

Technical factors

1. A new mine should
(a) be at least 13 km from another mine
(b) be able to mine coal from an area about 12 km by 12 km. A mine is limited to working an area this size because coal is not usually mined more than 6.5 km from the shaft. As underground transport travels at about 7 km an hour, the longest journey to the coal face would be one hour at the beginning and the end of a day's work. So on a 7½-hour shift, the miner would spend at most two hours travelling.

2. The deepest seam worked would be about 1,100 m deep. The depth of a coal mine is limited to about this depth by ventilation problems. In the exploration for the new coalfield at Belvoir it was found that at 800 m temperatures were 30°C. Working temperatures have to be kept below 25°C.

3. The new mine should be near an existing railway line. Most coal is moved by rail and the cost of building new lines should be kept to a minimum.

4. Seams less than 1 metre thick are not usually worth mining with modern machines.

Environmental factors

A new mine should be located so that it causes least disturbance to the people already living in the area and to the environment. To achieve this the following should be taken into account.

1. A mine should be at least 1 km from an existing village, and its waste tips should be at least 0.5 km from an existing village. The mine, its buildings and the waste tip will occupy most of a square kilometre.

2. A modern mine producing over 1 million tonnes a year will employ 1,500–2,500 men. With their families that will mean a new population of about 4,500–7,500 needing 1,500–2,500 new houses. If these houses are built in new villages this will involve the laying of expensive new water, sewage and electricity mains. If the houses are built in existing villages, what will be the effects of (a) building them all in one village or (b) spreading them out over several villages?

3. The mine should be located so that as little good farmland as possible is lost.

4. The mine should be located so that it causes little damage to important conservation sites.

4 The people of the West Midlands

Fig. 4.1. These are the crowds welcoming home the Aston Villa football team after it had won the European Cup in 1982.

Patterns on the ground

The first question a geographer would ask about the population is 'Where do the people live?' Altogether there are 5.1 million people living at an average population density of 3.9 people per hectare. That means that if all the people of the region were evenly spread out it would be roughly the same as four people (a small family, say) living on an area the size of a football pitch. But you know from your own experience that we do not live spread out like that. In some places we are crowded together in streets or flats, making up estates and towns and cities. In other places there is open countryside, with only a few farms and villages, and there are even more remote places with apparently no people at all.

One way that geographers try to make sense of this apparently haphazard picture is to draw a population distribution map. Fig. 4.2 shows the number of people in each of the districts of the counties of the West Midlands.

Key

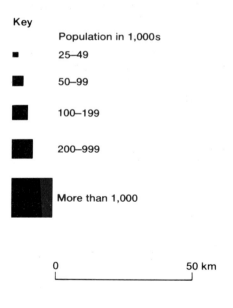

Population in 1,000s

- 25–49
- 50–99
- 100–199
- 200–999
- More than 1,000

0   50 km

See fig. 1.7 for district names.

Fig. 4.2. Population distribution in the West Midlands (by district) in 1981.

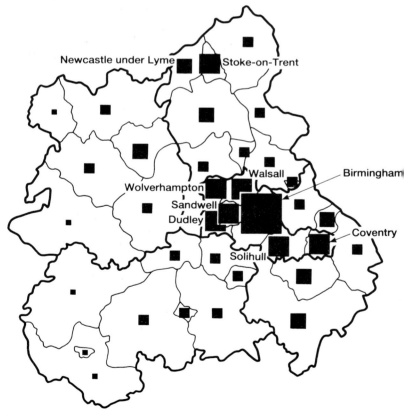

What does the map tell us about the pattern of population distribution? What can we say about the districts with the largest and smallest populations?

30

Table 8 *Population in the West
Midlands region, 1981.*

County	Population
Hereford and Worcester	630,218
Shropshire	375,610
Staffordshire	1,012,320
Warwickshire	473,620
West Midlands Metropolitan County	2,644,634
Birmingham	1,006,908
Coventry	314,124
Dudley	299,351
Sandwell	307,389
Solihull	198,287
Walsall	266,128
Wolverhampton	252,447

These seem to be the important points shown by the map:

(a) There is a small area where the population is more heavily concentrated than in the rest of the region. This high-density region corresponds very closely to the former West Midland Metropolitan County, which includes most of the large towns and cities in the region.

(b) The population density decreases as you move away from the area described in (a) towards the edge of the region.

(c) The **population gradient** is greatest to the west and south, but the gradient is much less as you travel northwards through Staffordshire.

(d) The western and southern fringes, in Warwickshire, Shropshire, Hereford and Worcester are much more sparsely populated.

The total population in each county is given in Table 8.

Cores and peripheries

This pattern consisting of a small area of dense population surrounded by a larger area of much sparser population, with a steep gradient between, is one that has been recognised in many parts of the world. It is so common that it has a special name: the **core-periphery model**. Geographers think it is so important because there are big differences in life-style between the core and the periphery. These differences are summarised in Table 10 on page 32. Most of the contrasts can be explained by differences in their settlement geography. Core areas usually have many towns and cities, while peripheries are usually rural. You can test this hypothesis in the West Midlands by checking if most of the towns and cities cluster together to form a core area. One way of doing this is to plot the distribution of all towns in the West Midlands listed in an AA Handbook, classifying them into the following size groups: 10,000 to 20,000; 20,000 to 50,000; 50,000 to 100,000; 100,000 to 1 million; over 1 million. Table 9 shows for each of the counties what percentage of the total population lives in towns of different sizes.

Table 9 *Urban population in the West Midlands region.*

	Percentage of the population living in all settlements larger than			
	100,000	50,000	20,000	10,000
Hereford and Worcester	0	21	48	55
Shropshire	0	42	42	48
Staffordshire	27	53	63	65
Warwickshire	0	27	45	58
West Midlands Metropolitan County	88	99.5	nearly 100	

Do you think this evidence supports the hypothesis of an urban core and a rural periphery?

core-periphery model

Geographers often use the term 'model' to describe in a generalised and simplified way complex patterns that are found in many different places. It is often possible to summarise the patterns in diagrams, like this one representing the core-periphery model.

Fig. 4.3. Core-periphery model.

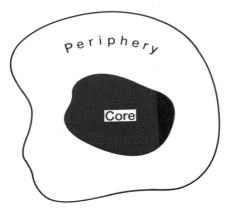

But geographers usually want to test if the model actually applies to the particular area they are studying. So we can set up the hypothesis that the core-periphery model is a good description of the population distribution pattern of the West Midlands. Because the patterns in a model are repeated in so many places, it usually means that similar causes or processes are at work. One of the reasons for studying geography is to understand these processes which affect our everyday lives.

Table 10 *A summary of the core-periphery idea, showing how it affects the lives of people in the West Midlands.*

	Cores	Peripheries
Settlement	High settlement density – people live in towns and cities. Housing costs are usually higher, but a wider range of houses available.	Low settlement density – rural settlement with people living in small towns, villages and farms.
Services	Big shops and supermarkets easy to get to, lower food prices. Doctors and dentists usually close by and several hospitals only a short journey away. Houses usually connected to mains electricity gas and sewers. Primary and secondary schools and colleges are all easily accessible.	Big shops only in nearest large town. Journey by bus or car to visit doctor or dentist. Hospitals usually further away; often difficult to visit patients. Mains electricity is usually available but not all houses have mains gas. Many houses have cess pits. Primary schools usually close by, but village schools often under threat of closure. Usually have to travel to nearest town for secondary school.
Recreation	Cinemas, theatres, museums, art galleries, sports centres and professional sports all easily accessible.	Better access to open countryside.
Transport	More frequent bus services operating for longer hours. Nearer to railway stations.	Poor public transport. Heavy reliance on private cars.
Work	Usually a wider range of jobs available in easy reach. Wages are generally higher.	Smaller range and number of jobs near to home. Usually have to travel to nearest town for jobs in shops and offices.
Health and welfare	Higher death rate and lower life expectancy. Higher death rates for bronchitis, lung cancer, TB and female suicide. Higher infant mortality. Higher crime rates.	Lower death rate and higher life expectancy. Lower infant mortality. Lower crime rates.

If you live in the West Midlands where would you go if you wanted to see the following: a live rock concert, a First Division soccer match, a county hockey match, the Motor Show, an Ideal Home Exhibition?

Apart from the differences between the core and the periphery summarised in Table 10, you could investigate other contrasts in people's lives. Figs. 4.8(b) and 4.10 might give you some ideas for a start.

The Birmingham–Black Country conurbation

You probably decided that what was the West Midlands Metropolitan County forms the core of the region. It consists mostly of an almost continuous urban area which has resulted from separate towns growing until their edges have met. Such an area is called a **conurbation**. The West Midlands conurbation is made of two closely linked parts. The eastern part consists of the city of Birmingham and the towns of Solihull and Sutton Coldfield. The western, Black Country part includes Wolverhampton, Walsall, Aldridge, Dudley, West Bromwich, Halesowen and Stourbridge. To the east, Coventry, which was also part of the West Midlands County, is separated from the conurbation by only a narrow belt of open country.

When you were testing the core-periphery idea you may have thought that Staffordshire did not fit into the idea as well as other counties do. You probably saw that this was because it contains two big towns: Stoke-on-Trent and Newcastle under Lyme. Although they are close to the edge of the region, they do not share the characteristics of a periphery. As we saw in chapter 1, they form an urban and industrial area, but on a smaller scale than the Birmingham–Black Country conurbation.

How can we explain the growth of the conurbation as the core area of the region? One way of answering that is to look at a process which geographers call **cumulative causation**. Some of the detailed steps of how the process works are set out in the flow diagram (fig. 4.4), and Table 11 illustrates the stages of growth of the West Midlands conurbation.

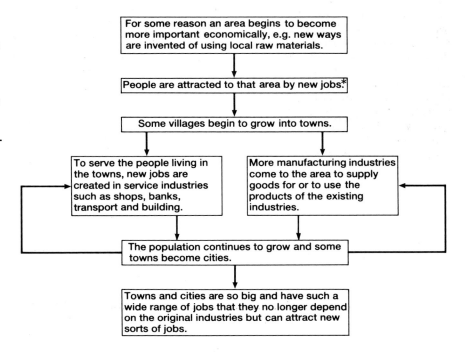

*Note: (i) People begin to leave rural areas and migrate to towns.

(ii) Migrants are often young and will have their families in towns.

(iii) Older people are left behind in rural areas and the population will grow less rapidly.

---

conurbation

The West Midlands is not the only area in Britain where a group of towns have grown together to form a conurbation. In the 1974 reorganisations of local government, the conurbations were made the basis of the new Metropolitan Counties. In 1981 the numbers of people living in them were:

Greater London	6.60 million
West Midlands	2.63 million
Greater Manchester	2.57 million
West Yorkshire	2.02 million
Merseyside	1.50 million
South Yorkshire	1.29 million
Tyne and Wear	1.35 million

About one-third of Britain's total population lives in conurbations. Use your atlas to find which towns and cities actually make up these conurbations.

cumulative causation

Once a town or a group of towns starts growing, the very fact that the town is there will act as a magnet to other people and industries, so that the town will continue to grow. This 'one thing leads to another' argument is often also referred to as a 'snowball effect'. The special geographical term used to describe the process is 'cumulative causation'. This is one of the processes which leads to the development of core-periphery patterns.

Fig. 4.4. Cumulative causation or the 'snowball effect' and how it can affect the growth of towns.

Table 11 *The development of the West Midlands conurbation.*

Coalbrookdale	The Black Country	Birmingham	Coventry
On Shropshire coalfield and with supplies of iron ore, limestone and clay	On South Staffordshire coalfield, with additional supplies of iron ore, limestone, clay and dolerite	Not on sources of any raw materials	Just to south of Warwickshire coalfield
1700–50 First use of coal to make coke for smelting iron ore by Darby here led to first modern iron industry in Britain	Coal mining only on a small scale using coal near to surface Metal industries carried out as domestic crafts	Domestic, craft-scale metal industries	Small textile industry, weaving ribbons
1750–1850 Metal and pottery industries continue but are already suffering competition from Birmingham and the Black Country	Rapid industrial expansion as new iron smelting methods spread to this area; new industries using the iron grow, as do industries using other metals Canals open as main type of transport for industry Heavy industry with smoke, soot and waste heaps give area its Black Country image	Rapid industrial expansion based on metal-using industries rather than metal-making, e.g. tools and guns Also an organising and market centre for industry Centre of canal network	Ribbon trade continues until collapse in 1850
1850–1900 Survives only as an isolated industrial area Coal mining becomes less important	Last phase of expansion with building of railways, but best coal is now used up and area begins to suffer from competition from newer industrial areas	Manufacturing continues to be important but its role as major city grows as service industries expand Now dominant town of area	Period of industrial depression
1900–present day Becomes almost derelict but attempt to renew economy by founding Telford New Town	Coal mining and metal production decline; the area is 'cleaned up' and metal-using industries become most important	The main commercial business and shopping city in region Britain's 'second city'	Industrial expansion based on motor industry and engineering Most rapidly growing town in region

Using the information in fig. 4.4 and Table 11, can you suggest:
1. why the conurbation became the core area?
2. how a sparsely populated periphery may be formed?
3. why Coalbrookdale didn't follow the 'snowball effect' path through fig. 4.4?
4. why it is important that some of the arrows follow circular rather than straight-line paths on fig. 4.4? What actual events do these circular paths represent in the case of the West Midlands?

One important idea that you should get from these diagrams is that the geography of the area is always changing. It still is, and we will now look at recent changes in the population of the West Midlands.

Population change

Whether populations grow or decline is controlled by a combination of two factors:

a) Natural change: If in one year more people are born than die, then there will be a natural increase, but if more people die than are born there will be a natural decrease.

b) Net migration: If more people move into an area than leave, then there will be net in-migration. If more people leave than move in then there will be net out-migration. (The words in-migrant and out-migrant tell you nothing about where the people have come from or where they are going to.)

Fig. 4.5. Population change in the West Midlands between 1971 and 1981.

Key

▨ Area where each census district lost population

▥ Area where each census district gained more than 5,000 people (i.e. areas where there was a large *absolute* increase)

░ Area where each census district gained less than 5,000 people but had an increase of over 5·0%. As the average increase for the region was only 0·5% these districts had a large *relative* increase.

0   50 km

Population changes in the West Midlands

Between 1971 and 1981 the total population of the West Midlands grew by only 27,000. However, that small increase hides many other changes which are important to an understanding of the geography of the region. These changes are summarised on fig. 4.5. We can only fully explain these changes when we have studied many other aspects of the geography, but we can start by looking at how migration and natural change are affecting the West Midlands.

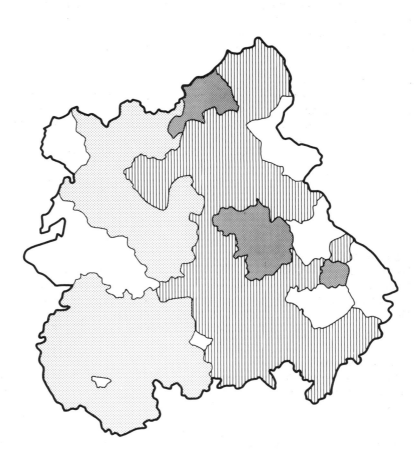

People on the move

After the first results of the 1981 census were published, the newspapers picked out one change which made the headlines: 'Census shows drift out of towns'. Most large cities and especially the conurbations lost population. If you look at fig. 4.5 you can see that this is true for the West Midlands region. With the exception of Solihull and Dudley it is the conurbation and the large urban, industrial areas which are losing population, while the areas immediately around them are growing most. Even the rural west is beginning to grow more rapidly. Much of this change is caused by people moving out of the large towns to live. You can see in fig 4.6 how builders and estate agents are trying to attract people to live in the country. But very often people do not move very far and may often **commute** to work in the large towns. This partly explains

35

commuting
The name used to describe travelling each day from the village or town where you live to another town, some distance away, where you work. Commuters (i.e. the people who travel this way) make up a large part of the morning and evening rush-hour traffic into and out of the large towns.

why the areas of largest population growth are spread out in a north–south belt through the region, because people are then able to use the M5 and M6 motorways for commuting. Some of the changes, as we shall see in chapter 7, are caused by the planned growth of New Towns at Redditch and Telford or by the expansion of towns like Tamworth.

We shall be coming back to these ideas later on but you might like to think about and discuss now the points listed below:

Luxury— with views of country

INTEREST has been high in a new, exclusive development in Cubbington, near Leamington.

The development, Austen Court, consists of 14 detached houses and bungalows, and stands on the edge of the village.

All the houses have superb views of the countryside, and the village church and vicarage are the backdrop.

The houses all have good-sized living rooms with feature fireplaces, separate dining rooms and utility rooms. Purchasers can choose

The Arlington

Fig. 4.6. How people are encouraged to live in the country. You could carry out a 'mini-census' of your own in the class or amongst friends and neighbours. Amongst the things you can find out are:

(a) Have they only moved within the town or village, or have they moved to the town or village from either another part of the country or from abroad? Work out how far they have moved.

(b) How long ago did they move?

(c) How many times have they moved house in the last ten years?

(d) Why did they move?

Discuss in class the best way of recording and analysing your results. How similar are the results of your 'mini-census' to those of the national census of 1981?

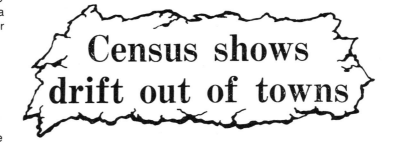

Census shows drift out of towns

1. Why do people want to move out of towns?
2. Why do they want to live in the country?
3. Does it make any differences to your chances of moving if you are fairly well off or not very well off? How might that affect which people move and which stay in the towns?
4. If these changes in population continued, what would happen to the core-periphery pattern?

Fig. 4.7. Population change in the West Midlands County.

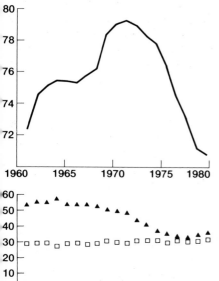

Key

—— Total population

▲▲▲▲▲ Birth rate

□□□□□ Death rate

Young and old: Big families and small families

The biggest change in population shown by the 1981 census was the fall in the number of people living in the West Midlands conurbation. What part did natural increase or decrease play in this change? If you look at fig. 4.7 you will be able to come to some conclusions about this.

1. What are the main trends in total population between 1961 and 1980?
2. What are the main trends in death rate and birth rate?
3. Does the graph show a natural increase or a natural decrease in population?
4. Does the rate of natural increase or decrease stay the same between 1961 and 1980?
5. What other causes of population change must be used to explain the fall in population after 1971? (Table 12 will help you.)

Table 12 *Population change in the West Midlands County.*

Year	Net out-migration (thousands)	Natural increase (thousands)	Year	Net out-migration (thousands)	Natural increase (thousands)
1961	4.0	24.0	1973	13.9	9.9
1962	9.2	26.2	1974	20.0	7.7
1963	23.5	25.4	1975	22.4	5.3
1964	25.8	27.7	1976	17.3	2.4
1965	25.9	25.3	1977	21.5	2.7
1966	15.8	24.4	1978	20.2	3.7
1967	20.8	25.4	1979	15.4	5.4
1968	1.1	24.2	1980	9.7*	7.9
1969	13.3	20.1	1981	7.6*	6.3
1970	17.7	20.1	1982	7.1*	6.7
1971	20.1	19.2	1983	10.0*	7.6
1972	16.2	13.1	1984	9.1*	7.5*

* Estimated figure.

Using the statistics in Table 12, draw a graph similar to the one in fig. 4.7 making sure that you can tell the difference between the lines for net out-migration and natural increase. Just as the distance between the birth rate and the death rate lines tells you how big the natural increase is, so the distance between your two lines will tell you whether the size of the natural increase is enough to make up for the loss of people by out-migration. Shade on your graph the periods when out-migration is bigger than natural increase. How do your results help to explain the trend in the change of the total population of the West Midlands County after 1971?

One factor that affects the ways in which birth rates and death rates change is the number of people who are in the child-bearing age groups. But also important are the number of children in a family. If you look at fig. 4.8 you will see some details of the age structure of three sample districts as well as of the whole region. The figures from the 1981 census are not in the best form for studying child-bearing age groups; most children are born to parents between 20 and 40, and there isn't a single set of figures for that group.

Fig. 4.8. Age structure of the population in the West Midlands, 1981:

For each of the districts how does the age structure of the population and the size of family explain the change in total population? Does migration seem to have had any effects?

(a) age structure of three sample districts.

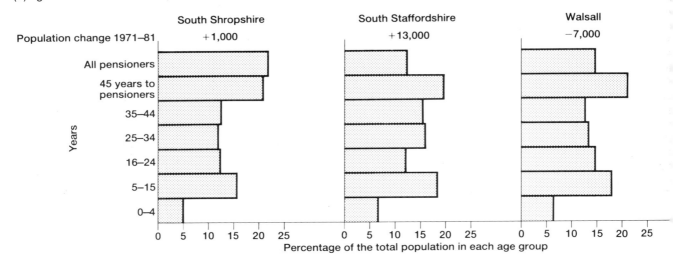

(b) distribution of young and old people, and large families.

Key

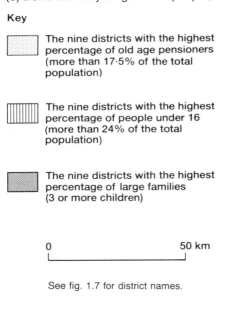

The nine districts with the highest percentage of old age pensioners (more than 17·5% of the total population)

The nine districts with the highest percentage of people under 16 (more than 24% of the total population)

The nine districts with the highest percentage of large families (3 or more children)

0   50 km

See fig. 1.7 for district names.

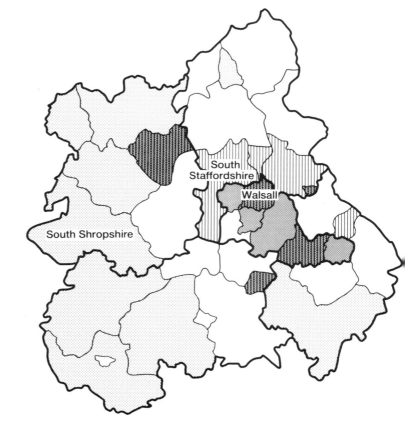

primary sector
All the industries which produce raw materials for other uses. Farming fishing, forestry, mining and quarrying are the primary industries.

secondary sector
All industries which make goods and result in an end-product for sale. This is sometimes called the manufacturing sector.

tertiary sector
All those jobs where people do not actually produce goods but perform services to keep other industries running; they provide services to people in everyday life. Work in shops and offices and running the buses are the sorts of jobs included here. This is often called the service sector.

People at work

What sorts of jobs do people do in the West Midlands? How does where people live affect the sort of job they have? Are their chances of being unemployed different if they live in one area rather than another? In order to collect information about them, jobs are put together in groups and in Table 13 there is a list of those groups which employ more than 50,000 people in the West Midlands. Lists like these can be very difficult to make much sense of, so we will look at some ways you can take it to pieces to make it easier to understand.

One way is to link together similar groups into sectors. The three sectors normally used are called **primary sector**, **secondary sector** and **tertiary sector**. Employment in the West Midlands in each sector is primary 3.0%, secondary 48.0% and tertiary 49.0%. There are only about 30,000 people employed in farming and about 25,000 in mining and quarrying; neither of these groups appears in Table 13. All the big employers are in the secondary and tertiary sectors. However, counting the number of jobs is not the only way of measuring the importance of an industry. You can also ask: 'How much does an area specialise in an industry?' or 'Is a particular industry more important here than in other places?' Table 13 includes those industries which in the West Midlands employ more people than the national average for those industries, and so you can pick out the industries which are especially characteristic of the West Midlands. We shall study them in more detail in chapter 5.

Table 13 *Employment in the main industrial groups of the West Midlands.*

	Number of people employed (thousands)	
Professional and scientific services (e.g. education, medical and dental)	304	
Distributive trades (e.g. shops and warehouses)	236	
Miscellaneous services (e.g. pubs, restaurants, sport, garages)	182	
Vehicle making (e.g. cars, aeroplane equipment)	180	*2.4
Metal goods (e.g. nuts, bolts, screws, tools)	168	*3.1
Public administration (e.g. local government offices)	125	
Mechanical engineering (e.g. machinery and machine tools)	121	*1.3
Metal manufacturing (e.g. iron and steel, copper and brass)	121	*2.5
Electrical engineering (e.g. electrical machinery, telephones, TV)	102	*1.3
Construction (e.g. house building)	102	
Transport (e.g. road and rail, air, post service)	98	
Insurance and banking, finance and business services	76	
Bricks, pottery, glass and cement	69	*2.7
Food, drink and tobacco (e.g. chocolate, bread and beer making)	55	

* Shows those industries in which the region employs more than the national average.
2.4 means that it employs 2.4 times the national average.

Where do people work?

So far we have only looked at the types of jobs for the West Midlands as a whole. But are all parts of the region the same? Fig. 4.9 will help to answer that. These are important ideas you can get from the graph:

(a) More than half the jobs are in the West Midlands conurbation.
(b) Although you have already seen that the primary sector does not employ many people anywhere, farming is relatively more important in Shropshire, Hereford and Worcester. Mining and quarrying is more important in Staffordshire.
(c) The service sector is an important employer in all the counties, but is relatively less important in the West Midlands conurbation and in Staffordshire.

Fig. 4.9. Percentage of workers in the West Midlands in each group of industries.

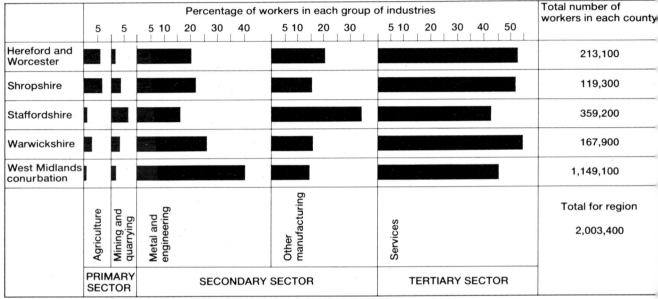

(d) On the other hand, the West Midlands conurbation and Staffordshire have a higher percentage of jobs in manufacturing.
(e) There is a heavy concentration of jobs in the metal and engineering industries in the West Midlands conurbation.

You might like to think about this in another way by discussing these ideas in class. Which counties seem to have a good balance of jobs in different sectors? Do any of the counties seem to have too many jobs in too few sectors? What are the dangers of not having a good balance of jobs?

The other side of the story about jobs comes when you look at where people are unemployed in the region. The pattern of unemployment is mapped in fig. 4.10. This map shows very clearly that it is the towns where there is a heavy dependence on the manufacturing sector that are suffering most. You can use the map to think back over some of the things you have learnt in this chapter.

Fig. 4.10. The percentage of men unemployed in the West Midlands in 1981.
Trace the outline of this map. Then, using two different types of shading, pick out those areas which have more than 15% unemployed and those areas which have between 10% and 14.9% unemployed.

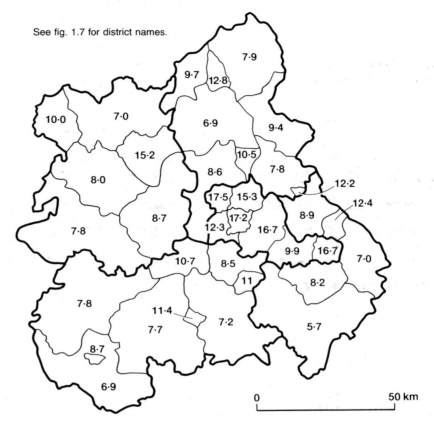

See fig. 1.7 for district names.

0   50 km

Do you agree with the following conclusions?
1. Unemployment is concentrated in the core area of the region. That is, the problem is worst in the West Midlands conurbation.
2. The rural periphery is suffering least from unemployment.
3. The industrial area of Staffordshire (Stoke and Newcastle) is an exception to the rule of lower unemployment in the periphery.
4. Areas which had large population growth between 1971 and 1981 are suffering high unemployment.
5. Places chosen as New Towns or Expanded Towns have high levels of unemployment.

5 Working in the manufacturing industries

In chapter 4 we saw that in comparison with Britain as a whole, the West Midlands and the Birmingham–Black Country–Coventry conurbation in particular, specialise in the metal, engineering and vehicle industries.

Industry in the news: the car industry

The car industry frequently makes the headlines (fig. 5.1), but the newspapers or TV often concentrate on the bad news. Is the car industry really so important that it should get all this attention?

Just consider these facts for a start:

(a) The motor industry (i.e. cars and commercial vehicles like trucks and lorries) makes up about 10% of the value of all manufacturing industry in the UK and is the second largest industry in the country.

(b) The motor industry is a major British exporter.

(c) During the 1970s it was the single biggest employer in the West Midlands, with about 8% of the workforce.

(d) About a quarter of the people working in Britain's motor industry live in the West Midlands.

So the motor industry is important both nationally and in the West Midlands. But its effect on the West Midlands is more complicated than can be measured by the numbers employed or cars produced.

One feature of industry in the Midlands is the way in which different industries are linked. These **linkages** are particularly extensive in the car industry, and the success or failure of that industry affects many industries and people in the West Midlands and in other parts of the country. This is another reason why it gets so much attention in the press and is a reason for looking at it in more detail now.

Fig. 5.1. Car firm in the news.

industrial linkage

Not all factories make finished products for sale to customers in shops. Many make goods which are supplied to other factories. The term 'linkage' is used to describe the trading connections which result from this flow of goods from one factory to another (fig. 5.2). The links by which a factory obtains its supply of raw materials or parts are called 'backward links'. (What do you think the term 'forward links' means?)

Sometimes all the linked factories are owned by one company, although the factories may be in different places. This is sometimes referred to as a vertically-linked system. In other cases, each factory is independently owned and may be in competition with others making similar products for the same markets. This is sometimes referred to as a horizontally-linked system.

Fig. 5.2. Industrial linkage.

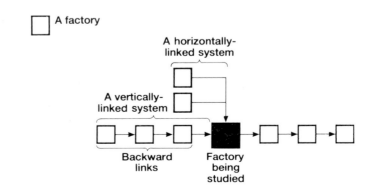

Rover Group plc

Motor vehicle makers, more often than many other firms, keep changing their names. British Leyland was renamed Rover Group in 1986 and is made up of smaller companies such as Austin-Rover Group, Freight Rover, Land Rover, Leyland Trucks and Buses and Unipart. Until recently it also included Jaguar Cars Ltd. This part of the chapter is mainly about Austin-Rover and Jaguar cars.

Rover Group plc

Austin-Rover (ARG) is the main motor manufacturer in the West Midlands, and its main product is cars. Cars are not made in one factory, but are assembled from components which may be made in many different places. The parts are transported by road or rail to another factory, where the car is put together on an 'assembly line' (fig. 5.3(a)). Assembly plants are large factories like the one shown in fig. 5.3(b).

Fig. 5.3.

a) Car assembly at Longbridge, Birmingham. This is part of the assembly line for the bodies of the Metro. Separate metal parts for the bodies are being welded together by robot machines. Once the bodies are assembled they then move on to the next stage to have engines and interiors fitted. These later parts of the assembly process need much more labour.

b) Austin Rover's Longbridge factory, on the south-western edge of Birmingham. The large building nearest the camera is where the bodies for the Metro are made. The main assembly lines are in the buildings at the top right of the photograph. Because of the heavy machinery used in a modern car factory, the buildings are only single-storey. As a result, car factories need a lot of space.

43

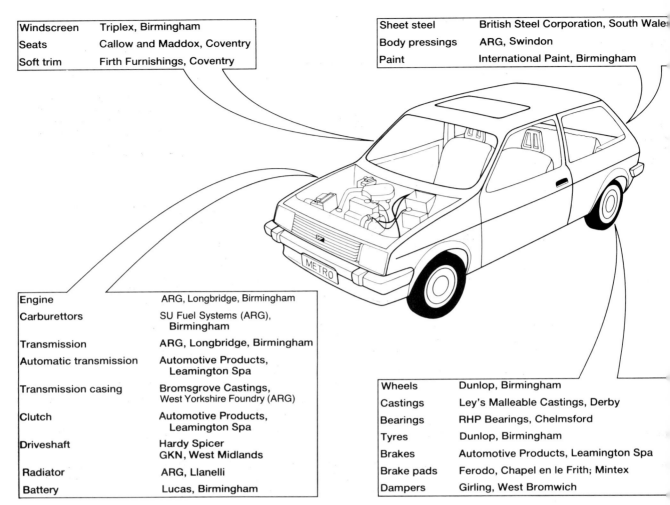

Windscreen	Triplex, Birmingham
Seats	Callow and Maddox, Coventry
Soft trim	Firth Furnishings, Coventry

Sheet steel	British Steel Corporation, South Wales
Body pressings	ARG, Swindon
Paint	International Paint, Birmingham

Engine	ARG, Longbridge, Birmingham
Carburettors	SU Fuel Systems (ARG), Birmingham
Transmission	ARG, Longbridge, Birmingham
Automatic transmission	Automotive Products, Leamington Spa
Transmission casing	Bromsgrove Castings, West Yorkshire Foundry (ARG)
Clutch	Automotive Products, Leamington Spa
Driveshaft	Hardy Spicer GKN, West Midlands
Radiator	ARG, Llanelli
Battery	Lucas, Birmingham

Wheels	Dunlop, Birmingham
Castings	Ley's Malleable Castings, Derby
Bearings	RHP Bearings, Chelmsford
Tyres	Dunlop, Birmingham
Brakes	Automotive Products, Leamington Spa
Brake pads	Ferodo, Chapel en le Frith; Mintex
Dampers	Girling, West Bromwich

Fig. 5.4. The supply of components for the Metro. This diagram lists the main components that make up the Metro and the location of the firms which make them.

The most important idea that you should get from studying figs. 5.4 and 5.5 is how interdependent all the factories are. However, the situation is even more complicated because each of the components factories also has chains of backward links. For Callow and Maddox to make seats for the Metro, it too must acquire from other firms the tubular steel frames, the springs, foam padding, plastic or cloth upholstery as well as adhesives, screws, nuts and bolts. Each of the firms which supplies these parts has suppliers in turn and in this way, eventually, thousands of firms are involved in the supply chain associated with the Metro. Add together all the different cars made by ARG and the other car producers and you can see why the vehicle industry affects so many people. If, for some reason, a car firm sells fewer cars, or if it has to close down, then the effects are felt by a lot of other firms, not only in the town where the factory is but over the whole country.

It should be clear that a successful car industry means that many other industries are also successful. But the British car industry is much less healthy than it used to be.

ig. 5.5. Location and size of factories owned by Austin-Rover and Jaguar.

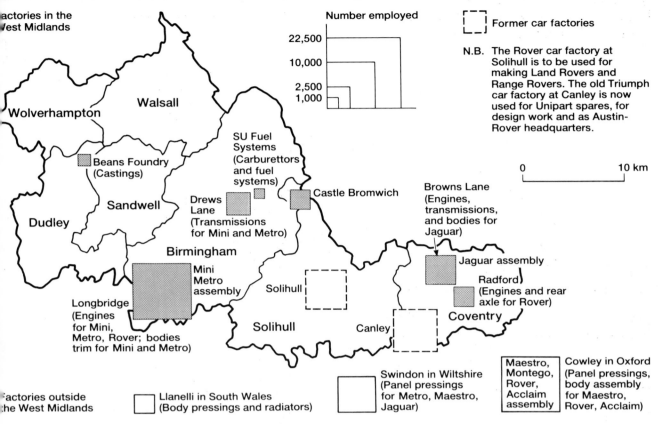

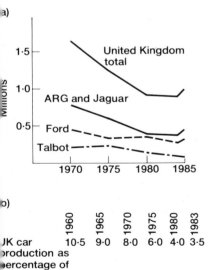

a) [graph]

1·5 — United Kingdom total

1·0 — ARG and Jaguar

0·5 — Ford

Talbot

1970 1975 1980 1985

b)

	1960	1965	1970	1975	1980	1983
UK car production as percentage of world production	10·5	9·0	8·0	6·0	4·0	3·5
Motor industry as percentage of total UK exports	16·9	15·9	14·4	13·1	8·6	5·1

Fig. 5.6. UK car production and trade: (a) car production in the UK; (b) figures for 1960–83.

In fig. 5.6 there are some data on the car industry. What do these data tell you about the size of the decline of the industry, and about the effect on different car firms? Can you suggest reasons for the decline?

In the next section we will look at how the decline of the car industry has affected Coventry, which is one of the main towns involved.

Coventry

As you can see in fig. 5.7, Coventry has been one of the most rapidly growing cities in Britain this century. Much of its growth is the result of the growth in employment in the motor industry there. Famous British car firms such as Triumph, Standard, Rover, Morris (all now in ARG), Hillman and Humber (now Peugeot-Talbot), Jaguar and Daimler, as well as older makes like Armstrong Siddeley and Alvis (which still makes military vehicles in Coventry), have had factories there. Massey Ferguson makes tractors, Carbodies makes taxis and Coventry Climax makes fork-lift trucks, and in the past aeroplanes and bicycles were made there, and there are also many component producers. It is possible to see in fig. 5.8 how dependent Coventry was on the motor industry. The graph shows that there were 54,000 people employed making vehicles in 1977. Since then the industry has been restructured and ARG has lost 12,000 jobs and Talbot 11,000 jobs. That means only about 30,000 people now work in the motor industry in Coventry – only 40% of the number in the industry in 1965, when it was in its heyday. You can also see from the graph that more than one worker in three was

45

in the motor industry in 1965. When such a large proportion of workers is in one industry, the economy of a town is said to be 'narrowly-based' and the town is over-dependent on that industry. If a recession hits that industry, employment is immediately affected and the life and economy of the town suffers as a result. The figures in Table 14 compare Coventry's unemployment rate with that for the West Midlands and Great Britain as a whole. These figures mean that in 1984 there were about 27,000 men and about 12,000 women out of work. What chances have they of getting jobs in Coventry? If you look at fig. 5.8 again you will see that the part of the economy in Coventry that was expanding

Fig. 5.7. Population growth and the car industry in Coventry.

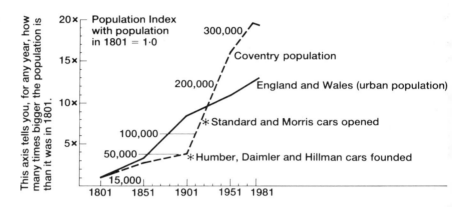

Table 14 *Unemployment in Coventry, the West Midlands and Great Britain.*

Unemployment rate at the end of	Coventry (%)	West Midlands (%)	Great Britain (%)
1984	17.4	14.0	11.9
1980	16.0	14.8	12.0
1975	5.4	4.7	4.5
1970	2.6	2.3	2.6

Fig. 5.8. Recent changes in the employment structure of Coventry.

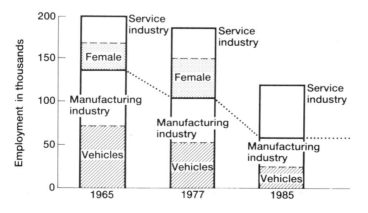

Employment in the motor industry in 1977

	Coventry	West Midlands	UK
Number in motor industry (thousands)	54	180	749
Total number employed (thousands)	185	2,202	22,619
Percentage in motor industry	29·1	8·1	3·3

was the service sector. The graph also shows that more women were finding jobs in services than men. In fact during the 1970s jobs for women were being created in the service sector as fast as they were being lost in manufacturing, so it was easier for women to get jobs than men. But think what the effect will be on office and shop jobs as more and more people lose their jobs and there is less money to spend. Another thing that fig 5.8 shows is that not all the jobs lost in manufacturing came from the motor industry. Other industries were in recession as well. This is partly because, as we have already seen, industries like engineering depend on the motor industry, and this has had its effect in Coventry. But big firms which were not part of the motor industry have also closed. One example is Renold Chains which employed over a thousand people. Many of these changes can be seen in the landscape of Coventry. Fig. 5.9 displays some of the evidence of these changes.

Fig. 5.9. The changing landscape of Coventry: (a) ARG office block. (b) 'Paint shop' where the bodies of Triumph sports cars were sprayed. After being empty for two years the factory was taken over by Peugeot-Talbot for Motorcraft spares, but as a result Motorcraft in Birmingham closed down. (c) An advertising hoarding.

(a)

(b)

(c)

Homes on sports field plan dropped

A FIRM has given in to city planners over the future of its sports ground in Coventry.

Renold Ltd., which closed its Coventry factory in 1980, wanted to use the 10-acre recreation ground at Tile Hill for housing, but the scheme was rejected by city planners.

47

What changes are taking place in the geography of Coventry as a result of the closure of factories?
Are the changes only affecting factory sites?
Are all the changes that the factory owners want, being allowed? Why do you think some of the factories and offices are still for sale or to let two years after they closed?
Are there any factories closing down near where you live? Perhaps you could investigate what is happening to them.

Patterns of industry

Not only is the idea of industrial linkage useful when looking at an individual industry like cars, but it can be applied in a more general way to the whole of the West Midlands metal and engineering industries. On fig. 5.10 you can see that these industries are sited in the core area of the region (see pages 31–32). The separate branches of these industries are linked as shown in Table 15. The starting point of the system of links is the metal-making industry. This is concentrated in the Black Country and particularly in Dudley and Sandwell. It grew up here using the raw materials and fuel produced on the South Staffordshire coalfield.

Fig. 5.10. The location of industry in the West Midlands.

Key

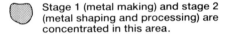 Stage 1 (metal making) and stage 2 (metal shaping and processing) are concentrated in this area.

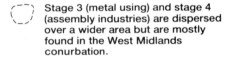 Stage 3 (metal using) and stage 4 (assembly industries) are dispersed over a wider area but are mostly found in the West Midlands conurbation.

■ Industrial satellite towns linked with the West Midlands metal and engineering industries.

∗ Other industrial towns where the main industries are not linked with the metal and engineering industries.

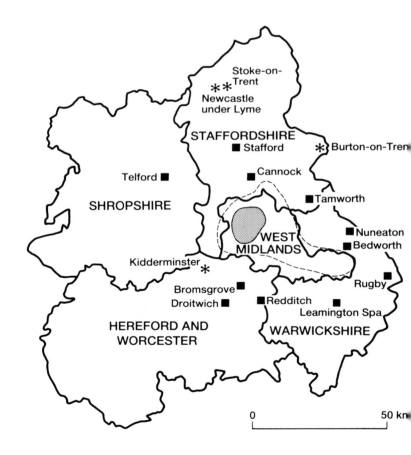

Table 15 *The industrial linkage system in the metal industries.*

Stage	Process	
1	Metal making	Smelting steel and non-ferrous metals: refining and alloying. The products are metal for use in the next stage.
2	Metal shaping and processing	Making castings, forgings and stampings. These are mostly sent on to stage 3, but there are some finished products like chains, brassware and saucepans.
3	Metal using	Metal is now made into recognisable products, e.g. central heating radiators, or into parts for use in stage 4, e.g. car components, gas rings, cooker panels and doors.
4	Assembly	Finished products are put together, e.g. cars, cookers, washing machines, lawn mowers, locks.

Table 16 *The iron and steel industry in the West Midlands.*

	1950	1960	1970	1980
Number of furnaces				
Blast furnaces	13	7	6	0
Steel furnaces	44	53	65	45
Output in thousands of tonnes				
Pig iron	560	560	660	0
Steel	870	1,580	2,080	540

If you look at fig. 5.10 again you can see that the further along the system of links you go the wider is the spread of the industries. So metal using, engineering and assembly work is done not only in the Birmingham–Black Country conurbation but also in small outlying industrial towns. The metal making part of the system has shrunk recently, as Table 16 shows. The last large steelworks, Round Oak in Dudley, closed at the end of 1982. The remaining steel furnaces are small and make steel by melting down scrap metal. As a result the West Midlands now has to import all its iron and much of its steel from the rest of Britain.

However, not all industry in the West Midlands is related to metals. You have already seen how important the pottery industry is in the Stoke-on-Trent–Newcastle conurbation. In addition that area makes tyres, textiles and computers. But it also has its share in the metal and engineering (especially electrical) industry, although here too the big Sheldon iron and steel plant has closed. Other specialisms of towns shown on fig. 5.10 are brewing at Burton and textiles and carpets at Kidderminster.

This jigsaw of industries making so many different products has led to the West Midlands being called the 'workshop of Britain'. Because it makes such a wide range of goods it has been able to remain a successful industrial area. If demand for one product collapsed, other industries

Fig. 5.11. Accessibility by motorway in Great Britain. Fig. 5.12. Areas receiving government aid to industry.

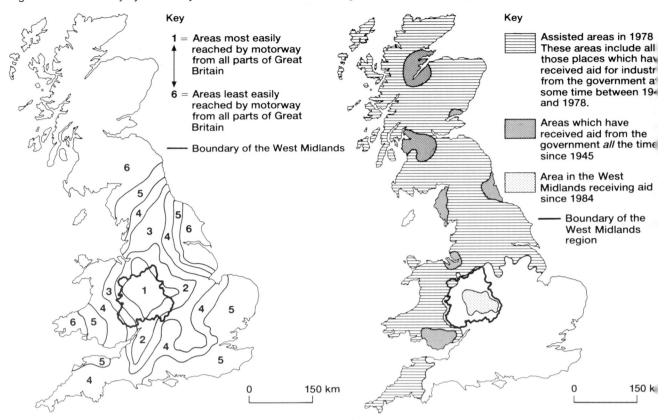

Key (Fig. 5.11)

1 = Areas most easily reached by motorway from all parts of Great Britain

6 = Areas least easily reached by motorway from all parts of Great Britain

—— Boundary of the West Midlands

0   150 km

Key (Fig. 5.12)

Assisted areas in 1978. These areas include all those places which have received aid for industry from the government at some time between 19– and 1978.

Areas which have received aid from the government *all* the time since 1945

Area in the West Midlands receiving aid since 1984

—— Boundary of the West Midlands region

0   150 km

accessibility and centrality

Accessibility is a word used to describe how easy a place is to get to. So a place with a high accessibility is easy to get to and a place with low accessibility is difficult to get to. Centrality describes the situation where a place is very accessible because it is centrally located.

were able to expand. Small factories making one product often changed to making something else. The region didn't have 'all its eggs in one basket' and the risk of being too dependent on a small number of industries was reduced.

A big advantage for the West Midlands is that the region is well placed to supply other parts of Britain with its products. It is centrally located on the British rail and motorway networks (see fig. 5.11) and therefore is **accessible**. A heavy goods lorry can reach the industrial areas of South Lancashire, Bristol and South Wales in two hours on the motorway. London and South Yorkshire are only three hours away. About 70% of the population of Britain lives within three hours' driving distance of the West Midlands. This **centrality** has helped make the region one of the most successful industrial areas in the country.

Other industrial areas in Britain have been much less successful than the West Midlands. The map in fig. 5.12 shows those areas of Britain which have had to receive government aid because they have problems caused by declining industries. Only the East Midlands, East Anglia and the South East have not had to receive such aid. In the West Midlands only the small peripheral area around Oswestry had high enough unemployment to get such aid. The rest was thought healthy enough not to need it. However, not only did the region not qualify for aid, the government took steps to prevent industry growing too rapidly there. It did this by controlling the location of new medium-sized and large factories. This was done by giving **Industrial Development Certificates** to firms if they wished to open new factories. They had to establish them at places which were approved by the government. It was very difficult to get an IDC to open a factory in the West Midlands. For example the new car factories that opened in the 1960s were in Scotland, at Bathgate near Edinburgh, Linwood near Glasgow, and in Liverpool. The effects of these controls can be seen in Table 17.

Table 17 *Job losses and gains in the West Midlands.*

	Number of jobs lost by firms moving out of the West Midlands	Number of jobs gained by firms moving into the West Midlands
1945–51	44,400	2,900
1952–59	15,800	4,100
1960–66	32,300	1,600
1967–71	17,100	1,000
1972–75	4,400	400
Total	114,000	10,000

Discuss with your neighbour or your teacher how you could use the figures in Table 17 to draw a graph to show the effects of the movement of firms on the number of jobs available in the West Midlands.

Jobs which might have come to the West Midlands went somewhere else. But an even more important effect was that the region continued to be heavily dependent on the metal and engineering industries. It got less than its fair share of new industries. As some of the old industries begin to decline, the effects are felt through the whole system because of the way the industries are linked. By November 1984 the situation was serious enough for parts of the West Midlands to qualify for regional aid for the first time. The area affected is almost identical to the Birmingham–Black Country conurbation.

Industry in the urban scene

These problems of industrial change can be studied in three small Black Country towns: Willenhall, Darlaston and Wednesbury, which lie across the Walsall–Sandwell district boundary.

A survey in 1980 asked industrialists what they thought about the difficulties of change, and their replies showed that there were three particular geographical problems. These are illustrated in fig. 5.13. However, despite such problems, changes are taking place to create new jobs and new places to work.

Fig. 5.13.

(a) Problem One: Not enough industrial land available.

To provide land for industry usually means knocking down factories which have closed down, like this bolt and nut factory, or building on derelict land, which is usually expensive to reclaim. The alternative is for new firms to move into old factories which are up for sale. At present the owners of this factory are trying to sell it to another firm.

(b) Problem Two: Poor factory buildings.

Many factory buildings in the area are old, small, short of space and crowded together. They are not suited to modern machines and production techniques. They are not attractive to work in. It is difficult and sometimes impossible to get large, modern lorries into them to deliver and take away goods.

(c) Problem Three: Poor local roads.

All the area is within 5 km of a junction on the M6 motorway and as a result has good links with other parts of the country. However, many of the roads which connect the factories to the motorway have not been improved. This also means that movement between factories is difficult. The narrow roads, like this one in the middle of Darlaston, often become congested.

New jobs for old

Although this part of the Black Country still relies heavily on metal working, the number of jobs in the industry is falling. The largest number of new jobs is being created in warehousing and distribution. Most of these jobs are found on industrial estates, such as the one in fig. 5.14, many of which have been built on what was derelict land or on sites where factories have been demolished. These new estates are pleasanter places to work than the old factories, but one problem is that they do not create so many jobs (see Table 18).

Fig. 5.14. Woods Bank Trading Estate, Wednesbury. This is a typical modern factory building on an industrial estate. Such estates are also called industrial parks and trading estates. In what ways is this building different from the one in fig. 5.13(b)?

This estate is built on the site of an old iron works and has a mixture of engineering and metal working (metal windows), factories and warehousing (Allied Carpets). Where there isn't enough space to build these estates in the existing built-up area, they are often built on the edge of the town. Do you know any examples of this in the area where you live?

Table 18 *Average number of people employed in different industries.*

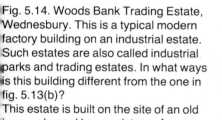

	Number of employees per hectare
Iron and steel	90
Metal goods and mechanical engineering	140
Light engineering	197
Warehousing and distribution	90

Look at the figures given in Table 18.
A typical industrial estate might cover 3 hectares.
If the site used to have 1 hectare of iron and steel industry, 1 hectare of mechanical engineering and 1 hectare of light engineering, how many people would have been employed?
If all the site is now used for warehousing, how many people are employed?
How many jobs have been lost?

An additional problem on industrial estates built at the edges of towns is that the workers may have further to travel each day to get to work. This will cost them more in time and money and they may be reluctant to go and work there. Very often industrialists don't want to move to the edge of the town either, because this may mean that they are further from their suppliers and customers.

In order to try to attract industry into the middle of towns, the government is co-operating with local authorities to set up special industrial areas called 'Enterprise Zones'. The one at Dudley was founded in 1981. In order to encourage factory building there, it has been agreed that industrialists do not have to pay rates for ten years and that they may pay fewer taxes. It is also much easier to get planning permission to build in these zones. This gives industrialists building there quite an advantage.

Can you think of any disadvantages?

6 Living in towns and cities

Patterns of housing

Have you ever thought about what sort of house you would like to live in when you set up a house of your own? What sorts of things would you look for? Before you read on, jot down a list of your ideas. There really is a lot to think about, including what you could afford, and your list has probably made you make some decisions not only about the house itself but also about the neighbourhood you would like to live in.

1. Would the house be old or new?
2. Would it be terraced, semi-detached, detached or a flat?
3. Would you want to rent a house or own your own? (People who want a council house or flat have to live in an area long enough to qualify, and have to have their name on the waiting list. People who want to buy usually have to earn enough to borrow the money they need from a building society or bank.)
4. How big would you want the house to be? Would it have a garden or a garage?
5. How near would you want to be to work, some shops, a school, a doctor's surgery and things like a park, a public house and a place of worship?
6. What did you decide about the **environment** of the area and the sorts of neighbours you would have? Which aspects of the environment do you think are important in choosing where to live?

environment
Those aspects of the surroundings which affect people's lives. It includes not only natural features but manmade ones as well.

One important factor which affects the type of house, the sort of neighbours and the environment of the area is the location of the place you live.

Where shall we live?

The photographs in fig. 6.1 illustrate four contrasting landscapes in a transect from the middle of Birmingham to its eastern edge. The areas in which the photographs were taken are shown on fig. 6.2.

A geographer is particularly interested in how and why areas are so different. One important factor which leads to the differences in these four landscapes is the age of the houses and other buildings. In most British towns and cities there is a distinct pattern in the way the houses of different age are distributed. This pattern is well developed in Birmingham and can be seen in fig. 6.2.

Fig. 6.1. Urban landscapes in Birmingham: (a) Ladywood; (b) Deritend; (c) Small Heath; (d) Sheldon.

One way of finding out how you would feel about living in different parts of Birmingham is to grade each photograph using this scoring system:

+2	beautiful	rich	interesting	friendly	quiet
+1	fairly beautiful	fairly rich	fairly interesting	fairly friendly	fairly quiet
0	neither beautiful nor ugly	neither rich nor poor	neither interesting nor boring	neither friendly nor hostile	neither quiet nor noisy
−1	fairly ugly	fairly poor	fairly boring	fairly hostile	fairly noisy
−2	ugly	poor	boring	hostile	noisy

You could add the scores for the class together to see how it feels about each area.
Do you all agree about which are the attractive areas and which are unattractive?
What is it in each area that makes you think it is attractive or unattractive?
Make a list of the good and bad points using the following headings: buildings, open space, traffic and roads.

Fig. 6.2. Age of buildings in Birmingham.

Key

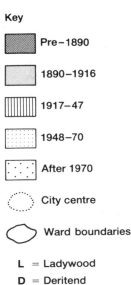

- Pre-1890
- 1890–1916
- 1917–47
- 1948–70
- After 1970
- City centre
- Ward boundaries

L = Ladywood
D = Deritend
SH = Small Heath
AG = Acocks Green
S = Sheldon

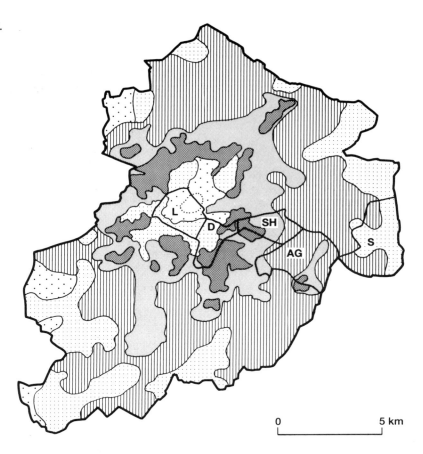

0   5 km

Look carefully at fig. 6.2 and make three or four imaginary journeys from the city centre in different directions, looking at the ages of houses along the lines you travel. Do you agree with the following conclusions about the distribution pattern of houses of different ages?

(a) There is a ring of pre-1890 houses in a zone about 1.5 to 3.5 km from the city centre.

(b) Beyond this there are houses built between 1890 and 1916. These houses don't form a continuous ring but they all lie within about 7 km of the city centre.

(c) By 1916 there was no more room for Birmingham to grow westwards because it had reached its boundary.

(d) A lot of houses were built where space was available, between 1917 and 1947. This filled almost all the space up to the boundary, particularly in the north-east and south-east.

(e) Between 1947 and the present there were more extensions to the area of houses, where space was available, especially in the south and south-west and in the east. By now building had reached all the boundaries.

(f) There is a ring of post-1947 houses lying between the city centre and the pre-1890 houses.

The pattern results from two processes in urban growth.

1. Outward growth.

As the population of Birmingham grew from 183,000 in 1841 to about 1 million by 1961, housing spread outwards from the old town centre. So the nearer to the edge of the city you get the more recently-built is the housing. Acocks Green only became part of Birmingham in 1911 and Sheldon in 1931. You probably also saw on fig. 6.2 that there are some areas of pre-1890 houses much further out than 3.5 km. These are the centres of old villages that were eventually swallowed up by the outward growth. They make exceptions to the rule about decreasing age with increasing distance from the centre.

2. Redevelopment.

Eventually some houses become so old that they have to be replaced by new ones. As the oldest houses are nearest the centre, most of the redevelopment will be near the centre. But eventually this rebuilding will spread like a wave outwards.

Can you see why?

The date when a house was built affects its type and style and what sort of neighbourhood it is in. We can draw a table using the photographs in fig. 6.1 and the information in figs. 6.2 and 6.3 to summarise these ideas.

Fig. 6.3. Housing conditions in a transect from the centre to the eastern edge of Birmingham.

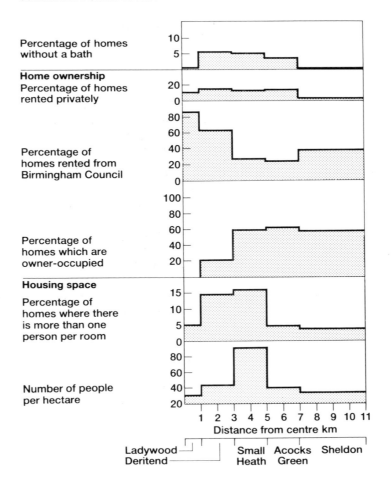

57

Rule six columns and four rows. Put the name of one of the photographs in the left-hand column of each row. Give the other columns the following headings: 1 Types of houses, 2 Housing space, 3 House ownership, 4 Description of environment, 5 Attractiveness score.
Can you see from this table and from the work you have done so far that where you live in a town will have a big effect on the sort of house and environment you will live in?

You can also look at it the other way round. Once you have decided what sort of house and neighbourhood you want, then you are more likely to find what you want in some parts of a town than in others.

Let's see how well this works for one of the decisions you have to make. If you wanted to rent a council house in Birmingham, you would need to know where your best chances of finding one would be. If you look at fig. 6.4 you can see that council houses have a very clear distribution pattern. There are two big concentrations. The first is in a block around the city centre, stretching as far out as about 3 km. The second is in estates found near the edge of Birmingham and lying more than 6 km from the centre of the city. Between these two concentrations a much smaller percentage of the houses is for rent from the council.

How would you describe the distribution pattern of houses to buy?

Fig. 6.4. Distribution of council houses and owner-occupied houses in Birmingham.

Key

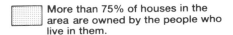
More than 75% of houses in the area are council houses.

More than 75% of houses in the area are owned by the people who live in them.

+   City centre

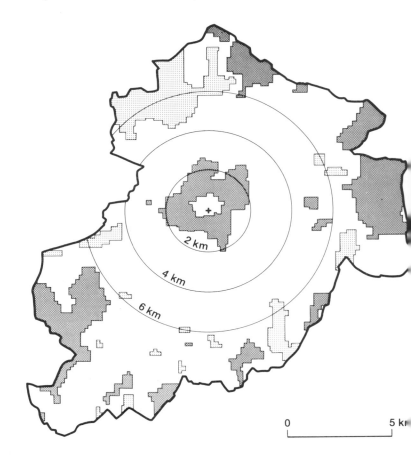

Who will our neighbours be?

One of the things that makes people feel at home is to have neighbours who are similar to themselves. You can investigate the relationships between where you might choose to live and the neighbours you might have. Fig. 6.5 and Table 19 summarise the social characteristics of people in different parts of Birmingham.

Key

More than 16% of the men who live here are unskilled manual workers.

More than 20% of the men who live here work as employers or managers.

More than 10% of the men who live here work in the professions (e.g. doctors, lawyers, accountants, lecturers).

+ City centre

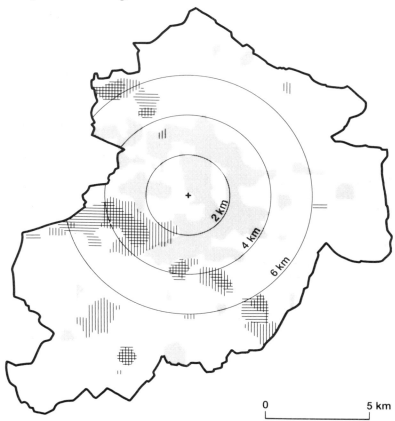

Table 19 *What might our neighbours be like?*

	Ladywood	Deritend	Small Heath	Acocks Green	Sheldon
Percentage of *people* living in the ward who are:					
Children under 16	21	30	31	20	6
Pensioners	20	9.8	11	20	19.8
Married women who work	64	45	39	60	62
Unemployed men	23.9	30.4	24.5	15	14
Unemployed women	12	11	8.8	7	5.8
Born outside the UK	16	35	35	11	5.7
Percentage of *families* living in the ward with:					
Only 1 adult	30	13	4.8	5.3	6
More than 3 children	5.6	17	20	7.3	5.3
A parent born in the New Commonwealth or Pakistan	18	44	47	8	2
No car	81	72	62	52	43

Use the statistics in Table 19 to draw a graph like the one in fig. 6.3 to show how some social conditions change from the centre of Birmingham to the edge.

1. Where would you be most likely to find neighbours who are pensioners; unemployed; immigrants; members of minority ethnic groups; working wives; who do not have a car; who have large families?
2. In which areas of Birmingham would you be most likely to find that your neighbour is an unskilled labourer; an owner of a factory; a member of one of the professions?
3. Can you use the map of the distribution of council houses and private houses (fig. 6.4) to help you explain the distribution of the homes of the people who do these jobs?
4. What conclusions can you come to about how where you live in the city affects the sort of job, the size of family, the age, the colour and the wealth of your neighbours?

social geography
That part of geography which studies the distribution patterns of different social and economic groups and how those groups affect or are affected by the environment in which they live.

These differences in **social geography** can be partly explained by people choosing to live in an area where they think they will be happy and at home.

An important factor in that choice is how well off people are. If a family has a lot of money, it will probably have plenty of choice where it lives. It can choose from more houses in lots of different areas and can afford to take time to find what it really wants. But the poorer a family is the less choice it will have and it may in the end be forced to take a house in an area that many other families have chosen not to live in. In this way, better-off families become segregated from poorer ones. Fig. 6.6 is a diagram that shows the ways in which some families will become concentrated into Inner City areas.

Fig. 6.6. A systems diagram of one set of residential segregation processes.

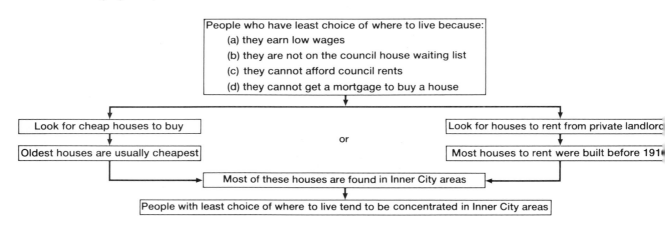

Small Heath: an Inner City area in Birmingham

Inner City areas

Those parts of towns and cities which usually surround the central shopping and business areas. They are areas of either old houses and factories (figs. 6.1(b), 6.9, 6.11) or houses and flats recently built to replace the old buildings (fig. 6.1(a)).

Now that Inner Cities are recognised as problem areas' they receive financial help. This is organised through specific government policies such as:

(i) Urban Aid Programme (1968)
(ii) General Improvement Area Policy (1969)
(iii) Housing Action Area Policy (1974)
(iv) Inner Urban Areas Bill (1978).

Inner City areas are now thought of as the major problem facing cities. Conditions in Ladywood, Deritend and Small Heath are typical of an Inner City. In the 1970s the social, environmental and economic problems of Small Heath were studied as part of a programme to try to bring about improvements in the area. Earlier in the chapter you looked at some statistical and map information. But this is not the only way a geographer can set about studying an area. Maps and figures give you *facts*, but it is often as important to know how people *feel* about an area. This is especially true if you are going to bring about changes which will affect the lives of the people who live there. Table 20 and fig. 6.7 give some of the results of the 1970s studies.

When the survey was done in Small Heath, people were asked what they particularly liked or disliked about the area. Table 20 sets out their replies, showing the percentage of people who mentioned each like or dislike.

Table 20 *Attitudes to living in Small Heath.*

Particular likes		Particular dislikes	
Good transport: easy to get to	34	Appearance of the area	18
Good shopping	32	Immigrants	16
People who live there	25	Area generally dirty	10
Convenient for work	17	Traffic and noise	10
Ties with area	13	Neighbours	6
Amenities	9	Lack of amenities	6
Good schools	7	Vandalism and crime	5
Peace and quiet	6	Neglect of streets and drains	5
Appearance of area	5	No facilities for children	3
House or flat	5	Poor parking	3
Rent or price of house	2	Poor shopping facilities	2
Healthiness of area	1	Problem families	2

Read all the material through and think about the following questions:
1. Why does Small Heath have a poor image?
2. What attitudes do the people of Small Heath have towards where they live? Do they all think the same about it? How will people's different attitudes make it difficult to plan changes in the area? Why do some of them want to move to other parts of Birmingham?
3. What image do the people of Small Heath think others have of them and the area?

Finding space for new housing

Actually finding space to build new houses is often a problem in the towns and cities of Britain. The diagram in fig. 6.8 summarises what sort of choice you might have if you wanted to move house in a city like Birmingham. We will now look at the processes that are changing the pattern of housing.

'Small Heath is such a drag. Look outside my front door and what do you see? Rubbish, absolute rubbish. . . I went out to Wythall with my mates and we were absolutely in our glory, because there was green beautiful grass . . . apples growing on the trees . . . acorns . . . .'

'These back alley houses look terrible and should be pulled down, but from the inside they are completely different. They are clean and tidy and the inhabitants are happy there.'

'If you go into town and tell people you're from Small Heath, they think you're living in a slum. I've got a teenage daughter and if she goes for an interview for a job and says she comes from Small Heath, her chances of the job have gone downhill.

'Just take a look at Edgbaston, Sheldon and places like that. There you would be happy knowing that you live in a clean environment. They probably think we're right rogues just because we live in Small Heath.'

Fig. 6.7. What people say about Small Heath.

'It's a very bad place to get jobs. But it's got worse recently because there was so many of the old buildings pulled down and the old small firms packed in.'

'My children have already decided for themselves. Not one of them wants to live in Small Heath. I don't believe in them flats at all, for the old people . . . I mean, they take them out of these back houses and they put them in these flats and they've got nobody, have they?'

suburb
A residential area found in the outer parts of towns and cities.

(a) Surburban expansion.

As outward growth is the most important process in the development of towns, the place you would expect to find new houses is in the outer **suburbs**. This process usually involves either the council or a private builder buying land that is probably farmland and using it to build houses, usually in large estates. There may be opposition to suburban expansion from both farmers and conservationists. One attraction of living in an outer suburb is that you are near the country. But the growth of the suburbs actually destroys the countryside. In some towns suburban growth has gone on until all the land within the town has been used up. If you look at fig. 6.2 you will see that this is the case in Birmingham. When this

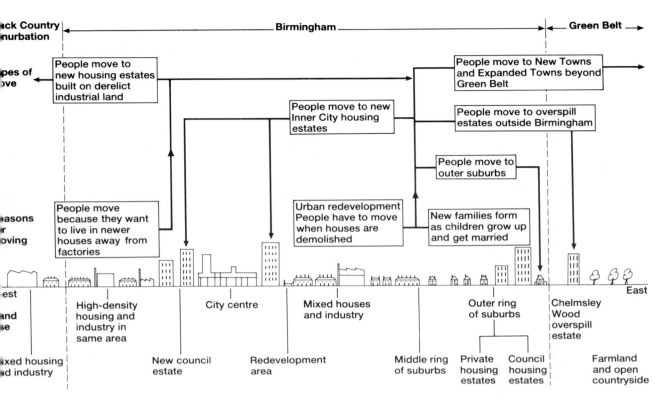

Black Country conurbation ← — **Birmingham** — → ← **Green Belt** →

Types of move

People move to new housing estates built on derelict industrial land

People move to New Towns and Expanded Towns beyond Green Belt

People move to new Inner City housing estates

People move to overspill estates outside Birmingham

People move to outer suburbs

Reasons for moving

People move because they want to live in newer houses away from factories

Urban redevelopment. People have to move when houses are demolished

New families form as children grow up and get married

West / **East**

| | High-density housing and industry in same area | City centre | Mixed houses and industry | Outer ring of suburbs | Chelmsley Wood overspill estate |

Land use

| Mixed housing and industry | | New council estate | Redevelopment area | Middle ring of suburbs | Private housing estates | Council housing estates | Farmland and open countryside |

Fig. 6.8. Finding space for new houses in Birmingham.

stage has been reached a town has to look for other ways of finding land for new houses.

(b) Infilling.

It is often possible to find small areas of land within the built-up area which can be used for houses. Often the land that has been unused for a long time has become derelict. Common sources of building land in the Black Country and in the Potteries are old factory sites and abandoned mines. This land is much less attractive than land in the suburbs. It is usually only available in small plots and so only small groups of houses can be built.

(c) Overspill.

By the middle of the 1960s land for new houses was already so short in Birmingham that it was necessary to try to find ways of housing people beyond the city boundary. This process is often called overspill. In the case of Birmingham it happened in three ways: (i) in new estates built just over the city boundary, (ii) in towns around Birmingham, and (iii) by the formation of New Towns. These schemes will be studied in chapters 7 and 8.

(d) Inner City redevelopment.

(i) Comprehensive Development Areas.

The oldest houses are found near the centre of towns. They may be so old that they become unhealthy to live in because they are damp or have poor sewers. They probably have outside lavatories, no bathrooms and no hot water. Eventually the houses may be left empty and derelict (fig. 6.9). Areas of such old and poor houses are often called slums. One solution to the problem of slum areas is to demolish all the houses and rebuild the area. Until about 1975 this was the solution in Birmingham to get rid of the worst areas nearest to the city centre. You can see the results

Fig. 6.9. Derelict housing in Sparkbrook, Birmingham. These houses will be left empty until they are knocked down to make way for redevelopment.
Why is it necessary to board up the windows?
What effects will it have on other people living in the area to have buildings like this nearby?

Fig. 6.10. Urban redevelopment in Sparkbrook, Birmingham. New houses built during the 1970s have replaced old factories and workshops. As a result of such changes the number of jobs in Inner City areas is decreasing and people living in these houses are having to travel further to work.
What attempts are being made to try to make this a more attractive place to live?

of this in fig. 6.1(a). The new buildings are mainly high-rise flats with some blocks of maisonettes and terraces of houses. Very often mixed in with the houses were old factories, and many of these have been demolished and replaced by houses (fig. 6.10). Comprehensive Development was very expensive. In the late 1970s the policy became less popular with planners and was replaced by the policy of renewal or improvement.

(ii) Urban renewal and urban improvement schemes.

Instead of demolishing all the buildings and starting from scratch renewal and improvement schemes involve the repair and modernisation of existing houses. This is what is happening in fig. 6.11. These changes are obviously a lot cheaper than building new houses, and this is the big advantage of these schemes. Another advantage is that people do not have to move to new areas of the city, which may be a long way from their workplace and their friends. Older people particularly like these schemes.

Fig. 6.11. Small Heath Park Housing Action Area. Old houses are being brought up to modern housing standards.

Patterns of shopping

Going shopping forms a part of everyday life in towns for most people. The provision of shops is one of the most necessary services that a town performs, and customers want shops to be located conveniently for the wide range of uses that they make of them. In Table 21 there is a summary of the shopping trips that one family made over the period of a few weeks. The table shows the types of things bought, how far the family went to buy them and how often they bought those goods. The more often the family used a shop the less distance they were prepared to travel for the sort of goods they bought there. The reverse is also true. The less frequently they shopped for a particular product the further they were prepared to travel. If this rule applies to most people, it gives a clue to understanding the distribution of shops.

It would be a good idea to check whether these rules apply to the members of your class. How could you do this?

Table 21 *Summary of shopping trips for a suburban family.*

Frequency of trip	Purpose of trip	Distance to shop
More than once a week	To buy bread, sweets, newspapers, food items run out of or forgotten	100 m
	To buy fruit and vegetables	800 m
Once a week	To draw family allowance and buy stamps	450 m
	To buy most of groceries and household items like washing powder, washing-up liquid, etc.	2.6 km
Once a fortnight to once a month	To get haircut/set	450 m
	To return library books	1.5 km
	To buy clothes and shoes	4.7 km
	To buy fish and chips	450 m
	To buy records	4.7 km
Infrequently	To buy chairs, table lamp	4.7 km
	To buy emulsion paint	800 m
	To compare washing machines	4.7 km
	To take watch for repair	4.7 km

Table 22 explains how the number of shops and the distance between them is related to (i) how often people use those shops and (ii) how far they are prepared to travel to them. One of the results of customers behaving like this is that a town will end up with a large number of small shopping centres and a small number of larger centres. In the large centres the shops we use less often are found grouped together.

The distribution pattern of shopping centres of different sizes in part of Coventry is shown in fig. 6.12, and as the map shows it is possible to classify them into a **hierarchy** according to how big they are and to what sorts of shops there are in them. As the centres are evenly spread out then the needs of the population for all their shopping should be met. Because such a hierarchy seems to be so efficient it has been used in planning the location of shopping centres. A good example of this is to be found in Redditch New Town.

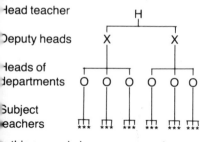
65

comparison and convenience shops

For many high-order goods people like to shop around comparing similar products in different shops before they buy. This explains why shops selling similar goods like shoes are often found close together in town centres. Planners call such shops 'comparison shops'.

Convenience shops are those which are easy to get to. They sell low-order goods like food, newspapers.

The Plan for the New Town said this:

'A three-tier hierarchy of shopping facilities is proposed. Occupying the top position in the hierarchy is the central area which should contain the major **comparison shops**, some **convenience shops** and a full range of other commercial, civic and social facilities.

At the second level it is proposed to establish district centres to cater for the weekly needs of the local population. These districts will vary in size and the centres will be located at bus stops.

At the lowest level of shopping activity it is planned to provide for the daily need of the population by means of "corner" shops, each conveniently located to serve some 300–400 families.'

Table 22 *A model of a shopping centre hierarchy.*

Distance to shops	People are prepared to travel only a short distance to shops for things they need often. Such goods are often called *convenience goods* or *low-order goods*.	People are prepared to travel a long way to shops for things that they do not buy very often. Such goods are called *high-order goods* and are usually either *durable goods* such as furniture or household equipment or *consumer goods* such as clothes or shoes.
Spacing of shops	Because people only travel short distances, these shops need to be close together in all parts of the town.	Because people travel longer distances these shops can be a long way apart and will draw their customers from a large part of the town.
Number of shops	Because they are close together and people do not travel very far to them there have to be a large number of shops to cover all the customers.	Because they are a long way apart there need to be fewer of these shops. As individual customers use them infrequently these shops need a large number of customers to get enough trade to stay open.
Size and location of shopping centres	These shops will be found in a large number of small shopping centres scattered through the town.	These shops will be grouped together in large shopping centres which are a long way apart.

Fig. 6.12. Shopping centre hierarchy in south-west Coventry.

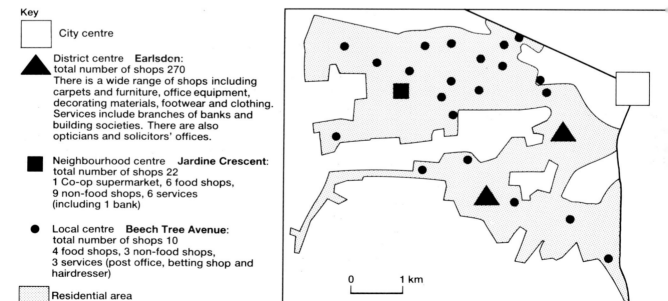

Key

☐ City centre

▲ District centre **Earlsdon:**
total number of shops 270
There is a wide range of shops including carpets and furniture, office equipment, decorating materials, footwear and clothing. Services include branches of banks and building societies. There are also opticians and solicitors' offices.

■ Neighbourhood centre **Jardine Crescent:**
total number of shops 22
1 Co-op supermarket, 6 food shops, 9 non-food shops, 6 services (including 1 bank)

● Local centre **Beech Tree Avenue:**
total number of shops 10
4 food shops, 3 non-food shops, 3 services (post office, betting shop and hairdresser)

▨ Residential area

0   1 km

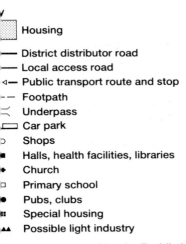

Housing

—— District distributor road
—— Local access road
◄— Public transport route and stop
-- Footpath
✕ Underpass
☐ Car park
○ Shops
■ Halls, health facilities, libraries
✦ Church
□ Primary school
● Pubs, clubs
⦂⦂ Special housing
▲▲ Possible light industry

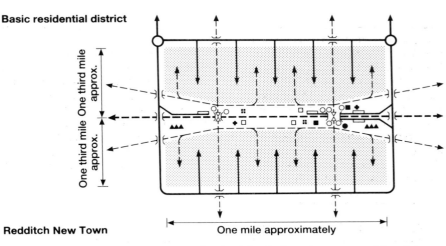

Basic residential district

One third mile One third mile approx.

One third mile approx.

Redditch New Town

One mile approximately

Fig. 6.13. Part of the Plan for Redditch New Town.

Fig. 6.13 is a map from the Plan for Redditch showing one residential district.

Can you identify on the map the district and local shopping centres?
What other facilities are provided at the centres?
How have the planners tried to make the district centres the focus of community life for the residential district?
How have they tried to reduce the amount of traffic at the shopping centres?

Perhaps you think this sort of hierarchy seems to be too well organised and efficient to be true. We do not always shop in such a predictable way and go to the nearest shops. We might be put off by poor parking facilities or attracted by good ones. We might do a lot of our shopping on the way home from work or be attracted to a centre because we like a particular shop or product we can get there. However, the pattern does mean that there are usually shops easily accessible no matter how we want to do our shopping.

How well do your family's shopping habits fit in with the hierarchical pattern?

At some time or another most people need and want to go shopping in the city centre. Birmingham city centre is at the top of the shopping hierarchy for the whole of the West Midlands.

Birmingham Central Business District

The statistics in Table 23 give some information about shopping in central Birmingham, the highest-order centre in the city's hierarchy.

Table 23 *The number and relative importance of different types of shop in the central area of Birmingham.*

Type of shop	Number of shops	Percentage share of money spent in town centre
Grocery	8	3.2
Other food	36	2.7
Newsagent, sweets and tobacco	63	2.7
Clothing and footwear	211	36.6
Household goods	54	7.0
Other non-food shops	89	12.3
General or department stores	12	35.0
Total	473	100

67

Central Business District

The name given to the area in the middle of a town which has the main shops, offices and important public buildings. Very often when people talk about 'going shopping in town' or 'going to town' they mean they are going to this central area. You might have heard the American name for the same area: downtown.

Fig. 6.14. Birmingham's Central Business District.

Key

1 The New Street shopping complex: an indoor shopping area built above the main railway station

2 Bull Ring Shopping Centre: an indoor shopping area occupying several floors and completely traffic-free

3 Birmingham Post and Mail newspaper offices

4 Large department store

5 Bank of England building

6 St Philip's Cathedral

7 Market buildings:
These have been demolished since the photograph was taken. What are the disadvantages of having the wholesale markets at the edge of the CBD?

8 Lancaster Circus

9 St Martin's Church

10 The Rotunda office block

How could you use these statistics to show that:
  (i) low-order goods form only a small part of the trade;
 (ii) high-order goods form the largest part of the trade;
(iii) comparison goods are more important than durable goods;
(iv) the amount of money spent in particular types of shops is not related to the number of those shops?

These figures are typical of a high-order centre and suggest that shopping is concentrated on a small range of shops and types of products. The success of these shops depends on their being able to attract a large number of customers from the whole city. The central location at the focus of the road network makes it the most accessible place for the largest number of people.

However, this also makes the city centre an attractive location for other activities. These too serve the whole city and include the council offices, the law courts, main public buildings such as the museum, prestige head or regional offices for banks and insurance companies, and big cinemas and theatres. Because the city centre has these additional activities, the area where they are all found together is often called the **Central Business District** (CBD). The photograph in fig. 6.14 is of Birmingham's CBD.

This photograph illustrates many of the features associated with Central Business Districts. Use it to make a simple sketch and neatly add some notes to your sketch to show that you can recognise those features listed here.

(a) Because so many different users compete for land in the city centre, land is in short supply and is expensive as a result. Land is therefore used as intensively as possible. This is done by having tall buildings to create a lot of floor space on a small amount of land; by replacing old and small buildings by new ones; and by combining different uses of the land in the same area.

(b) Different types of use tend to concentrate together in particular areas.

(c) A disadvantage of the accessibility of the area is that it suffers from traffic congestion. Attempts to remedy this have included building a ring road to divert traffic from going through the centre; raising shopping areas above ground level and separating them from traffic; and creating pedestrian-only areas.

Meeting our other needs

The people who live in towns not only need homes and places to work and shop; they also have to be provided with a wide range of other services, such as recreation, education and health care amongst others. These services too have distinctive geographical patterns.

A city like Birmingham, Coventry or Stoke-on-Trent has many different educational facilities. There are primary schools, secondary schools and colleges of further education which meet the needs of the inhabitants, and also universities and polytechnics which attract students from all over this country and from abroad. It is possible to think about these different types of establishment as a hierarchy:

serve small area	serve medium-sized area	serve large area
low threshold population	medium threshold population	large threshold population
large number evenly dispersed or spread	relatively few at accessible places in their service areas	very small number at accessible location
low-order	middle-order	high-order

Where would primary schools, secondary schools, colleges of further education and universities and polytechnics fit into this hierarchy? The actual numbers of each type in Coventry are:

Primary schools	125	Colleges of further education	4
Secondary schools	21	Universities and polytechnics	2

Why would you expect primary schools to be found in all parts of the city?
Why might a college of further education or a polytechnic be near the city centre?

The map in fig. 6.15 shows the location of two different aspects of leisure and recreation in Birmingham.

Can you explain the differences in numbers and locations of parks, open spaces, theatres and cinemas?
You could investigate the distribution of some other services in a town you know. Could you test the following hypothesis, for example: Doctors' and dentists' surgeries are common and are evenly distributed throughout the town but there are few hospitals and they are centrally located? A useful source of information for this would be the telephone directory. Can you think of any other patterns you could investigate using either the Yellow Pages or the telephone directory? If you do try out a project like this you could check your results to see if any parts of the town are badly served.

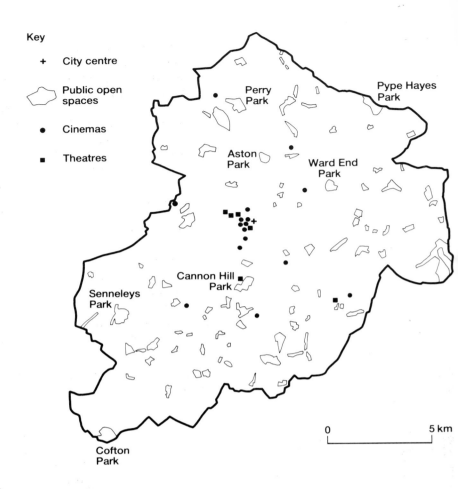

Fig. 6.15. Areas of parks and public open spaces, and cinemas and theatres in Birmingham.

Key

+ City centre

⬭ Public open spaces

● Cinemas

■ Theatres

Perry Park

Pype Hayes Park

Aston Park

Ward End Park

Cannon Hill Park

Senneleys Park

Cofton Park

0   5 km

Competing for space

We have now seen that there are many ways in which land in a town can be used. Space is needed for houses, factories, offices, shops, schools, parks, hospitals and many other things. All these uses compete for land. So far we have looked at these aspects of the geography of a town as separate features. We will now see how they all fit together.

You already know that one part of a town looks quite different from another part of the same town. One area might consist of houses, a few shops, a pub on the corner and a small park. Another area is recognisable by its factories with their storage yards, loading bays and car parks. There are no houses and very little open space. Geographers call these clearly recognisable areas in towns 'functional zones'. Each functional zone has a typical mixture of land uses. It is possible to draw a map which summarises the layout of the functional zones in a town or city (fig. 6.16).

Similar patterns are found in a lot of towns, which suggests that there must also be some regularly recurring causes of the patterns.

(a) As most towns grow outwards from the centre, the older buildings are near the middle and the newer ones near the edge.

(b) The shape of most towns means that there is less land available in the centre than there is near the edge, and therefore many potential users compete for land in the centre.

(c) The location of a functional zone affects its accessibility and its accessibility affects the type of use found there. However, accessibility changes with time. Before 1918 there was little public transport and it was expensive. Most people had to live near where they worked. As more public transport was developed after 1918 it was easier to travel further to work. After 1950 more people began to own cars and this made it possible for more people to choose to travel even further to work.

(d) The character of functional zones is affected by how much their development was controlled by planners. Before 1918 there was very little control of land use. Building was in order to make a profit for the builder, the owner and the landlord. This led to land being used very intensively. Between 1918 and 1945 there were still relatively few controls but Local Authorities became house builders for the first time, and council housing estates began to appear. After 1945 land use began to be planned in zones. Four processes were particularly important: (i) the creation of separate zones for industry and housing to prevent pollution; (ii) the allocation of large blocks of land to either council or private housing; (iii) the demolition of the areas of oldest housing to be replaced by council housing; (iv) the rebuilding of town centres.

Could you use these ideas to explain either the functional zones of Birmingham (fig. 6.16) or another town you know well?

Fig. 6.16. The functional zones of Birmingham.

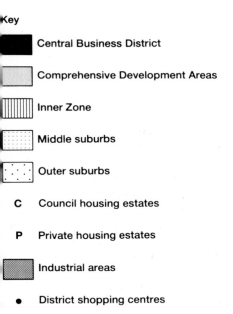

Key

■ Central Business District

▦ Comprehensive Development Areas

▥ Inner Zone

▦ Middle suburbs

▦ Outer suburbs

C   Council housing estates

P   Private housing estates

▦ Industrial areas

●   District shopping centres

○   Neighbourhood shopping centres

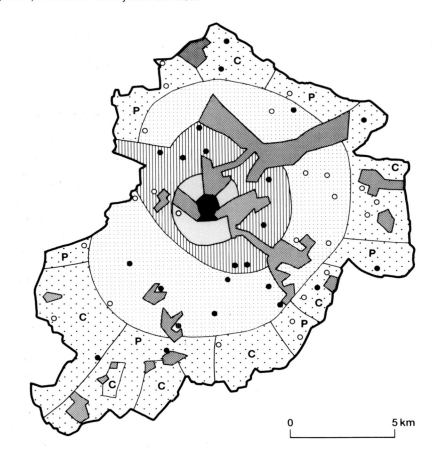

0   5 km

7 The urban system

Are all towns the same?

The towns we have studied in earlier chapters of this book have grown because of the development of industry. Their prosperity still depends on industry. The towns also provide for the needs of the people who live in them through shops, offices, hospitals, schools, sports clubs and parks. In other words, the towns provide a range of services for their population. These towns are located on the coalfields. They take up only a small area in the West Midlands region and are concentrated in the Birmingham–Black Country and Potteries conurbations.

If you look back to page 4 you will see that there are also towns outside the core area. These towns are different in two ways from the industrial towns:

(a) They are smaller.

(b) They are more scattered or dispersed.

We will now examine what role these towns fulfil. Fig. 7.1 is a dispersion graph which shows how much shopping space there is for each inhabitant in the towns of the West Midlands. There are some very big differences. The towns of the conurbation have between 0.3 and 0.7 square metres per person. The people there are adequately served by shops, so we could say that up to 0.6 or 0.7 square metres per person is 'normal' and will meet the needs of the inhabitants. So those towns with more than 0.7 square metres per person seem to have more shops than the people who live there need. How do these shops make enough money to survive if there are so many of them? The towns with this apparently spare shopping capacity are the small, scattered, non-industrial towns. They supply goods and services not only for their own people, but also for the people who live in the surrounding country areas. Because of this, these towns are often called service centres.

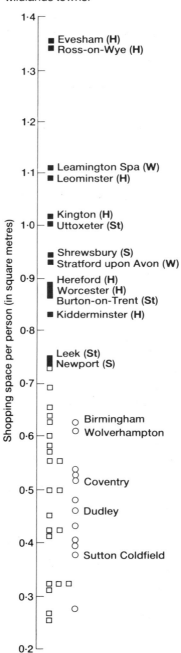

Fig. 7.1. Shopping space in West Midlands towns.

Key

■   Main service centres

○   Towns in the conurbations

□   Other towns

Counties in which
main service centres are situated
are indicated by initials as follows:

H = Hereford and Worcester

S = Shropshire

St = Staffordshire

W = Warwickshire

Table 24 Shops and services in the main shopping area of Evesham.	
Grocery (incl. International, Tesco)	4
Other food	15
Newspapers/cigarettes and tobacco, confectionery	7
Clothing and footwear	24
Household goods	19
Other non-food goods	21
General stores (Boots, Woolworth)	2
Other services (banks, building societies, cafés, offices, e.g. auctioneers, estate agents)	39
Total	131

Table 25 Employment in Evesham.	
	%
Primary	10.9
Manufacturing	21.8
Construction	7.2
Gas, electricity and water	3.6
Distributive trades	13.8
Miscellaneous services	13.1
Public administration	6.5
Other services	22.6

Evesham – a rural service centre

Evesham is a small country market town with a population of 15,200. It lies in the midst of the rich agricultural land of the lower Avon Valley. The farmers of this area specialise in growing fruit and vegetables. As well as being the market town for these farmers, Evesham is also the administrative centre for Wychavon District in the Hereford and Worcester county. It is an attractive town to live in and its residential population grew by 10% between 1971 and 1981. It does have some manufacturing industry. Some of it is totally unrelated to the farmland around. For example, there is one firm, Willmotts, which makes spectacle and presentation cases, and another makes household furnishings and fabrics; but food processing (Robirch Sausages and Pies) and small agricultural engineering workshops have direct connections with farming. However, the chief function of Evesham is to provide services for its own population and that of the surrounding area.

Look at the information in fig. 7.2 and Tables 24 and 25. Can you find evidence to support the following statements about Evesham?
1. Most of the employment is in the service sector.
2. Shopping facilities are dominated by high-order shops which provide consumer and durable goods.
3. In a small town a large amount of space is given over to shopping.
4. Most of the land in areas with factory-type buildings is used for activities which provide services for farmers.
5. The shopping area is spread out along the main streets, as is the case in most country market towns.

Fig. 7.2. Air photograph of Evesham.

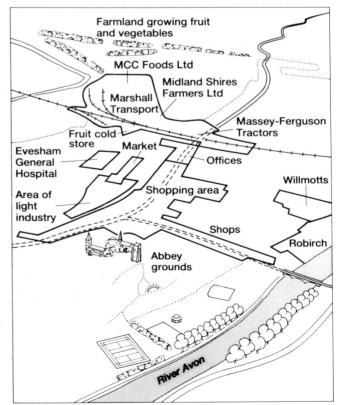

	The percentage of all services in Shropshire found in each town
Albrighton	1.20
Bishops Castle	0.89
Bridgnorth	3.00
Brosely	1.00
Church Stretton	1.10
Cleobury Mortimer	0.96
Craven Arms	1.14
Ellesmere	1.72
Knighton	1.25
Ludlow	3.30
Market Drayton	3.40
Much Wenlock	0.99
Newport	3.10
Oswestry	5.80
Shifnal	1.70
Shrewsbury	16.10
Telford	14.20
Tenbury Wells	1.30
Wem	1.60
Whitchurch	2.80

low-order, middle-order and high-order service centres

Low-order service centres: Towns providing low-order goods and services which the people in the surrounding areas need most often and for which they are not prepared to travel very far. As each one supplies only a small number of goods and services it receives a relatively small income and so can support only a small population.

High-order service centres: Towns providing high-order goods and services which the people in the surrounding areas need least often and for which they are prepared to travel a long way. In an area the size of a county there is usually enough business to keep only one high-order centre profitable. This is usually the county town and supports a large population.

Middle-order service centres: Towns of intermediate importance between high- and low-order centres.

In addition to being a service centre, Evesham has also become a tourist centre, as have many market towns in the West Midlands. Because the towns have been markets for many centuries, they usually have many historic buildings. Most of the shops are in old buildings because the town centres have not been redeveloped as they have in most of the industrial towns. It is these historic features which attract tourists. In Evesham the River Avon also adds to the tourist activity, as there is a lot of holiday traffic along the river. There are moorings along the river bank and the town is a convenient shopping place.

One problem is particularly associated with Evesham and many of the other market towns. This is the problem of traffic congestion.

Can you make a list of the reasons why congestion is such a problem in towns like this? Very often it is suggested that a by-pass is the best solution to the problem. Who are the people who would support building a by-pass and what would their argument be? Who might argue against it and why?

A system of service centres

If we studied all the other small country towns we would find that they are also service centres for the surrounding rural areas. But are all the service centres in any area the same? Table 26 shows the results of a survey that was recently carried out in Shropshire. The towns are in alphabetical order and it is difficult to make much sense of the list.

Use the information in Table 26 to draw a dispersion graph similar to the one in fig 7.1. Your vertical scale will be 'Percentage of all services in Shropshire'. Now try to interpret the graph. Are the towns scattered equally on the graph, or do they fall into groups, with gaps between them? If they fall into groups, is there the same number of towns in each group? Compare your ideas with your neighbour.

The geographers who did the original survey divided the towns into three groups. They put the gaps between Telford (14.20%) and Oswestry (5.80%) and between Whitchurch (2.80%) and Ellesmere (1.72%).

Is that the conclusion you came to? If it isn't, do you think their results are better than yours or would you be prepared to support your decision?

The three steps are another example of a hierarchy (see chapter 6, page 65) which divides the towns into **low-order**, **middle-order** and **high-order service centres**. The hierarchy is mapped in fig. 7.3.

By having towns from different levels of the hierarchy spread all over the county, people living anywhere in the county should be able to buy all the goods and services they need and can afford. When all the towns work together in this way, each town playing a particular role or function, geographers usually call it 'an urban system'.

For the urban system to work well, you have to be able to travel easily into the towns. A large part of England's 'A' road network was developed from old tracks and highways which were used by country people to take their goods to market. A town's position on the 'A' road network often reflects its position in the urban service system, so by measuring the accessibility of a town, one can assess where it fits into the urban hierarchy. Fig. 7.4 is a simplified road map of Hereford and Worcester, with all the 'A' roads shown as straight lines when they connect two towns directly.

Fig. 7.3. The urban hierarchy of Shropshire.

Key

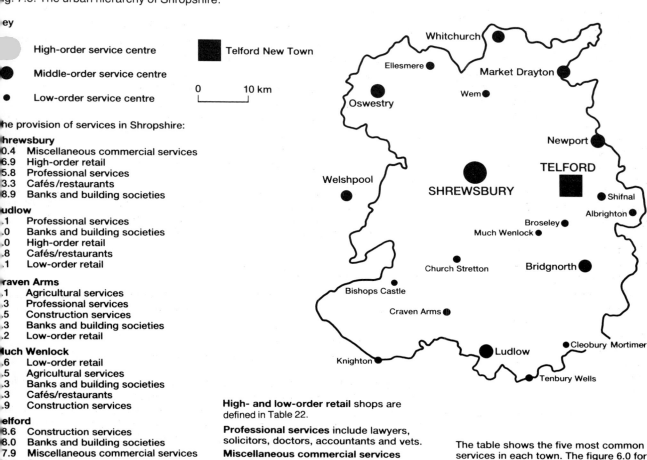

⬤ High-order service centre   ■ Telford New Town

● Middle-order service centre

• Low-order service centre

0   10 km

The provision of services in Shropshire:

Shrewsbury
10.4   Miscellaneous commercial services
6.9   High-order retail
5.8   Professional services
3.3   Cafés/restaurants
8.9   Banks and building societies

Ludlow
.1   Professional services
.0   Banks and building societies
.0   High-order retail
.8   Cafés/restaurants
.1   Low-order retail

Craven Arms
.1   Agricultural services
.3   Professional services
.5   Construction services
.3   Banks and building societies
.2   Low-order retail

Much Wenlock
.6   Low-order retail
.5   Agricultural services
.3   Banks and building societies
.3   Cafés/restaurants
.9   Construction services

Telford
8.6   Construction services
8.0   Banks and building societies
7.9   Miscellaneous commercial services
7.7   Schools
6.2   Garages and transport

High- and low-order retail shops are defined in Table 22.

Professional services include lawyers, solicitors, doctors, accountants and vets.

Miscellaneous commercial services include all offices not in any other category.

The table shows the five most common services in each town. The figure 6.0 for banks in Ludlow means that Ludlow has 6% of the banks in Shropshire.

Fig. 7.3 and the tasks related to it show how the urban system works in Shropshire.

Draw a column graph showing the number of towns at each level of the urban hierarchy.

Work out the average distances between all the low-order centres. For this exercise, remember that middle- and high-order centres will also be used as low-order centres by people who live near to them.

Work out the average distance between all the middle-order centres. Don't forget that people living near Shrewsbury will use it as a middle-order centre.

What is the relationship between the number of centres at each level and the distances between them?

The area from which a town is able to attract people to use its services is called its **sphere of influence**. What is the relationship between the size of the sphere of influence and the position of the town in the urban hierarchy?

If you were a farmer living near Craven Arms, what use would you make of Shrewsbury, Craven Arms and Ludlow? Why might you want to go to Birmingham sometimes?

Sphere of influence
The area from which a town is able to attract people to use its services.

75

Fig. 7.4. The 'A' road network of Hereford and Worcester.

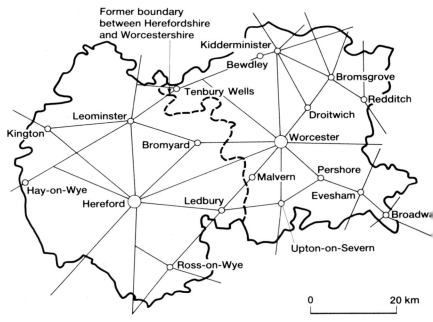

You can use the map to measure the accessibility of the towns marked. For each town count the number of roads joining it to all other towns. This will give you a simple Accessibility Index. So the index for Kington is 3, as it has three road links. The index for Bromsgrove is 5. Work out all the index figures and then draw up a table of results, putting the towns in rank order of accessibility. Can you use that table to suggest which are the high-order centres and which are low-order? Are all parts of Herefordshire equally accessible?

When the counties of Hereford and Worcester were merged in 1974, Worcester became the county town. Does this map suggest why it was chosen in preference to Hereford?

One of the effects of a town being a high-order centre with a good level of accessibility is that it becomes an attractive place to work. This encourages commuting from the surrounding rural areas and can lead to traffic congestion in and near these towns. It can also lead eventually to higher-order centres growing at the expense of lower-order centres. The commuting pattern for Hereford is shown in the statistics in Table 27.

Table 27 *The daily movement of people to work in the county of Hereford.*

Into Hereford		Out of Hereford
From		To
	Other towns	
410	Leominster	20
180	Ross-on-Wye	20
	Rural Districts	
650	Leominster and Wigmore (N)	0
300	Bromyard (NE)	50
310	Ledbury (SE)	50
380	Ross and Whitchurch (S)	20
2,080	Dore and Bredwardine (W)	170
820	Weobley (NW)	20
3,820	Hereford	1,590

(Letters in parentheses indicate the direction of the Rural Districts from Hereford.)

Can you design a diagram which will show how many people move into and out of Hereford each day and show where they come from?

The West Midlands urban system

One of the advantages of towns forming an urban system is that the whole area should be provided with all the services it needs. A good question to ask is 'Is the West Midland region well served by its urban system?'

To start to answer that question, you must remember that the urban system for the whole region contains not only the rural service centres like the ones we have just been studying; it also has all the industrial towns we studied in chapters 5 and 6. The scattergraph (fig. 7.5) is a summary of all the parts of the whole urban system.

When all the towns in the West Midlands are studied together as a system, there seem to be some problems with the way it is working. In earlier parts of this book we have seen that the industrial towns in the system face difficulties. They can be summarised like this:

(a) A large part of the total population is concentrated into a few large industrial towns. We have called this the core area of the region.

(b) There are problems in finding enough space for houses in these core towns.

(c) Many of the factories are old and are in congested locations.

Fig. 7.5. Rank-size distribution of towns the West Midlands.

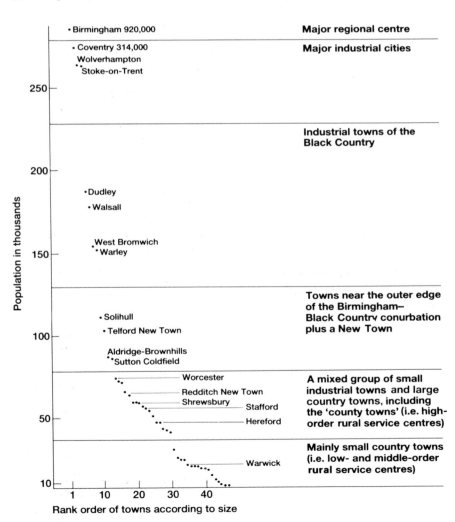

decentralisation

The name given to a policy which tries to move power, people or things from an area in which they are concentrated into other areas so that they are more evenly spread. Decentralisation is often used to overcome the disadvantages of core-periphery patterns.

Other examples of decentralisation in the book are (i) the movement of people in chapter 4; (ii) the movement of industry onto town-edge industrial estates in chapter 5; (iii) the movement of people into suburbs in chapter 6.

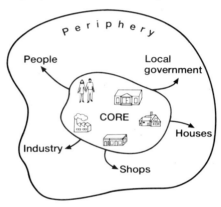

Fig. 7.6. Decentralisation.

One solution to these problems is to move people and industry out of the crowded areas into other towns. This policy can be called **decentralisation**. The effect of decentralisation is to increase the size of the smaller towns in the system which are chosen to receive the people. The changes which were planned are shown in fig. 7.7. You can see from the map that two types of change were involved. Some towns were chosen to become 'Expanded Towns'. These were usually rural service centres and the plan was to enlarge them. This did not involve big changes to the existing town, but rather a speeded-up growth.

The other type of change was to develop two 'New Towns', Redditch and Telford. These were planned where there were existing small but declining industrial towns. The new growth involved such large changes that the resulting towns are very different from the ones they replaced. Your teacher may have a collection of materials from the Development Corporations. You could use these to investigate how successfully the New Towns have brought about change in the West Midlands urban system.

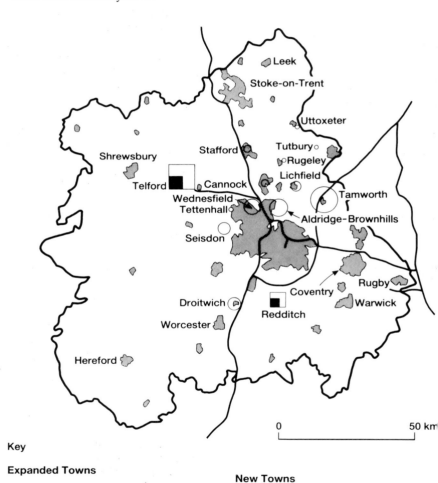

Key

Expanded Towns

Proposed number of dwellings to be built

5,000
2,500
1,000
100

Motorways

New Towns

Proposed population
Original population

Thousands
250
50
0

Major built-up areas

Fig. 7.7. Changes planned in the urban system of the West Midlands.

Tamworth: an Expanded Town

In 1967 the West Midlands Economic Planning Council published a report called 'The West Midlands: Patterns of Growth'. In it Tamworth was chosen to be one of the towns to receive people who were being moved out of Birmingham as part of the decentralisation policy. Because the planners thought that Birmingham and other towns were 'full up' they used the word 'overspill' to describe the population movement. It was rather insensitive to give such a name to a group of people.

Tamworth received its overspill during the 1970s. Some of the changes this brought about can be seen by studying figs. 7.8 and 7.9, which show that the overspill scheme was successful in moving people. Indeed, Tamworth was the third most rapidly growing town in England between 1971 and 1981. However, the scheme was less successful in creating new jobs. Tamworth was already a small industrial town before the scheme started. It had metal and engineering factories, including the small car firm making Reliant three-wheelers and Scimitars. New engineering firms have been opened and the wholesale supply, distribution and service sectors have grown. Most of these new firms are located in modern industrial estates; but Table 28 shows that there are not enough jobs in Tamworth. Even if all the jobs went to people living in Tamworth, 10,000 would have to find work outside Tamworth. But the position is worse than that. Some of the jobs in Tamworth are held by people who live in the area around Tamworth. This means that even

Fig. 7.8. Tamworth overspill scheme: (a) Changes in Tamworth during the time of the overspill scheme. (b) A comparison of the age structures of the existing population of Tamworth and the overspill population.

(a)

	1966	1981	Effects of overspill scheme	Percentage change 1966–81
Population	32,000 plus expected natural increase by 1981 6,000	64,000	+ 26,000	+ 100
Houses and flats	10,658	21,513	+ 10,855	+ 102
Jobs	12,000	18,500	+ 6,500	+ 54

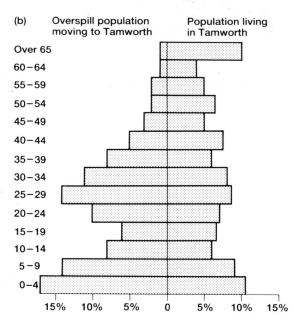

(b)

What would the population of Tamworth have been (approximately) in 1981 if there had been no overspill scheme?

What are the main differences between the age structures of the existing population of Tamworth and the overspill population?

What services would be particularly in demand in Tamworth to provide for the needs of the newcomers?

What evidence is there to suggest that the provision of houses was able to keep pace with the growth in population?

What evidence is there to suggest that the provision of jobs was not able to keep pace with the growth of population?

(a)

(c)

Fig. 7.9. Tamworth: (a) a shopping street in Tamworth town centre; (b) a new indoor shopping area in Tamworth town centre; (c) late nineteenth-century houses in the inner residential zone of Tamworth; (d) a new housing estate and secondary school on the edge of Tamworth.

What evidence is there in these photographs of recent changes in the urban geography of Tamworth?

One way to tackle the question is to look at changes in
– the town centre
– the inner zone of old houses
– the edge of the town.

Another way to tackle it is to ask what new services are needed to support the much bigger population.

more people who live in Tamworth have to look elsewhere for jobs. Most of these people commute to Birmingham each day. It has been harder to decentralise jobs than people. One of the reasons for this in manufacturing industry is the idea of linkages we looked at in chapter 5.

If a firm has lots of forward and backward linkages with other firms which are located nearby, it may be reluctant to move to a new area. Secondly, many of those people who commute, work in offices. We saw in chapter 6 how important an accessible location in central Birmingham was to many of these offices, and as a result it is difficult to decentralise the office jobs.

Table 28 *Employment and unemployment in Tamworth.*

Employment in Tamworth in 1981	
Economically active population (i.e. people working or wanting jobs)	28,500
Number of jobs available in Tamworth	18,500
Number of people who have to go outside Tamworth to work	10,000
Unemployment in Tamworth In April 1981 the unemployment rate was 12.2%	

In March 1982 there were 6,111 people unemployed but there were only 66 vacancies. If there are 6,111 unemployed out of an economically active population of 28,500, can you work out the unemployment rate?

8 Living and working in the countryside

Farming

Fig. 8.1 is of a typical Midlands farming landscape. The house has a huddle of farm buildings round it and lies at the end of a track connecting the farm to the road. The buildings are surrounded by a pattern of fields, which are separated by hedgerows out of which trees grow. The fields are put to a variety of uses. In some fields cereal crops such as wheat and barley have been grown and can be recognised by the scattered piles of stubble. Others have grown grass, which has been harvested for **animal fodder**. Grass in other fields is being grazed by sheep or cattle. Only a few hundred metres away lies another farm which is run in a very similar way. This sort of farming is called mixed farming. It gets this name because the farm depends on a mixture of different activities – growing cereals and grass as well as rearing animals. The way these activities fit together in the running of the farm is shown in fig. 8.2.

Use the questions in the caption to fig. 8.2 to help you follow the links in the system. When you have done that draw a sketch based on the photograph in fig. 8.1 to summarise the main features of mixed farming. Use the description above to help you.

animal fodder

Grass grown on farms is used in two ways, as pasture or as fodder.
Grass is called pasture when it is grazed directly in the fields by the animals.
It is called fodder when it is cut during the summer and stored for use in winter. This is done in two ways:
(a) The grass can be dried and used as hay.
(b) It can be stored undried in a large airtight pile or pit and allowed to ferment; this process turns it into silage.

Fig. 8.1. A mixed farming landscape near Stratford upon Avon, Warwickshire.

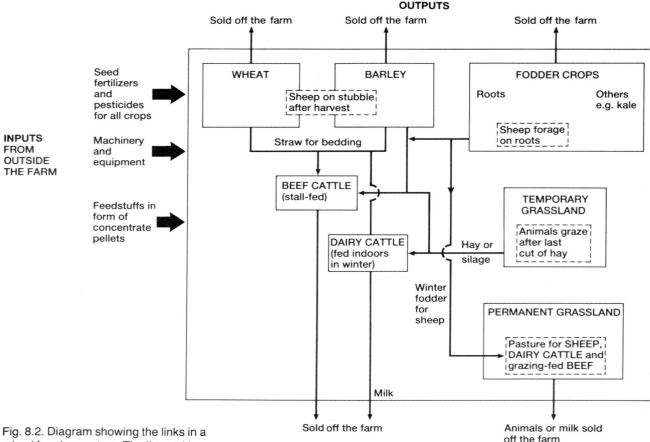

OUTPUTS

Sold off the farm   Sold off the farm   Sold off the farm

INPUTS FROM OUTSIDE THE FARM

Seed fertilizers and pesticides for all crops

Machinery and equipment

Feedstuffs in form of concentrate pellets

WHEAT

BARLEY

Sheep on stubble after harvest

FODDER CROPS

Roots   Others e.g. kale

Sheep forage on roots

Straw for bedding

BEEF CATTLE (stall-fed)

DAIRY CATTLE (fed indoors in winter)

TEMPORARY GRASSLAND

Animals graze after last cut of hay

Hay or silage

Winter fodder for sheep

PERMANENT GRASSLAND

Pasture for SHEEP, DAIRY CATTLE and grazing-fed BEEF

Milk

Sold off the farm

Animals or milk sold off the farm

Fig. 8.2. Diagram showing the links in a mixed farming system. The lines with arrows on the diagram show the ways in which the crops and animals are used on the farm.

Follow through the diagram the ways in which wheat, barley, fodder crops, temporary grass and permanent grass are used. (Temporary grass is grown in rotation with the other crops and so the field may have grass growing in it for one or two years at a time. Permanent grassland refers to those fields where grass is left for seven years or more.)

Work out where beef cattle, dairy cattle and sheep get their food from.

What products does the farmer sell?

Which items on the diagram will the farmer have to buy?

What other expenses is he likely to have?

However, not all these activities are carried out on all farms. In some parts of the West Midlands, farmers tend to specialise in some aspects at the expense of others. The information in fig. 8.3 shows how farming varies from one part of the region to another.

You can use the land use and land quality information to produce a summary of the main features of farming in each county. For Staffordshire you might write

'Staffordshire has very little high-quality farmland and a lot of low-grade land. This poor land is found in the north-east of the county and is associated with the higher land of the Pennines and the moorland edge. Most of the farmland is of average quality. As a result Staffordshire has the lowest proportion of arable land (i.e. cereals, fodder crops and temporary grassland) in the West Midlands. Most of the farmland is used for pasture. This is used for animal rearing of which dairy farming is the most important.'

Write similar summaries for each of the other counties.

. 8.3. Quality of farmland and types of farming.

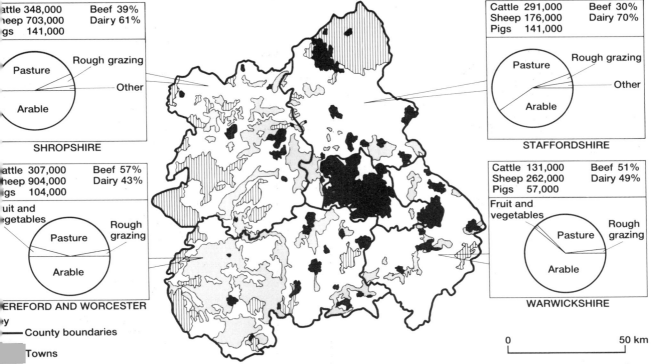

attle 348,000   Beef 39%
heep 703,000   Dairy 61%
gs   141,000

Pasture   Rough grazing
Other
Arable

SHROPSHIRE

Cattle 291,000   Beef 30%
Sheep 176,000   Dairy 70%
Pigs   141,000

Pasture   Rough grazing
Other
Arable

STAFFORDSHIRE

attle 307,000   Beef 57%
heep 904,000   Dairy 43%
gs   104,000

uit and
egetables
Rough grazing
Pasture
Arable

EREFORD AND WORCESTER

Cattle 131,000   Beef 51%
Sheep 262,000   Dairy 49%
Pigs   57,000

Fruit and
vegetables
Rough grazing
Pasture
Arable

WARWICKSHIRE

0   50 km

y
County boundaries

Towns

Grade 1 and 2 farmland This land has few or no limitations to agricultural use. A wide range of crops can be grown, including the more difficult vegetables. Yields are consistently high. This land gives the farmer maximum choice of activities.

Grade 3 farmland This is average quality land on which the range of crops is comparatively limited. Grass and cereals are the principal crops and they give reasonable yields under average management. The land supports some of the best quality pasture.

Grade 4 and 5 farmland This is land with severe limitations due to adverse soil, relief or climate, or a combination of these. A high proportion of the land will be under grass, some of which will be only of rough grazing quality. Very few other crops are found and this land gives farmers little choice of activities.

Farmers make decisions

You will see from your summaries that all the activities in fig. 8.3 are found in all the counties. But different activities get more emphasis in one county than in another. How do farmers decide which aspects of farming to concentrate on? Fig. 8.4 will help to explain their decisions. How much choice a farmer has in the type of farming he does is very much affected by the physical conditions of the area in which his farm is situated. You could make a hypothesis that 'the better-quality the land is, the more choice the farmer has: the poorer-quality the land is, the less choice the farmer has'. The physical conditions that affect the quality of farmland are (i) the amount of rainfall, (ii) temperatures, which influence length of growing season and speed of plant growth, (iii) soil, and (iv) how steep slopes are. You will probably remember from other parts of your geography course that all these factors are usually related to the height of the land. There is a summary of that relationship in fig. 8.5.

Fig. 8.3 shows that most of the poor-quality farmland in the West Midlands is found in the western parts of Hereford and Shropshire and in the north-eastern parts of Staffordshire. These are the areas where

83

Fig. 8.4. A model of the farming system.

Factors affecting how a farmer decides to run his farm

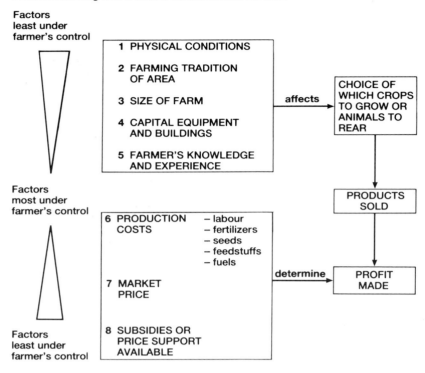

Fig. 8.5. Physical conditions and quality of farmland.
Can you make up a diagram like this to show how low land can give good-quality farmland?

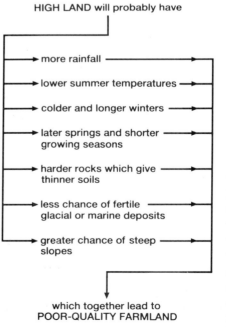

high land and heavy rainfall coincide (fig. 8.6). In the highest and wettest parts of these areas farming is restricted to sheep rearing and to raising beef cattle to be sent to lower areas for fattening. There is almost no arable farming. So in these areas the farmers have virtually no choice in the type of farming they do. In the lower parts of these poor areas it becomes possible to add dairy farming to the choice of activities.

In the lower, warmer and drier parts of the West Midlands you find the better-quality farmland and in these areas any combination of mixed farming activities is possible. However, even in these areas it is not easy for farmers to keep changing what they produce. This is because of the factors 2 to 5 in fig. 8.4. Let's take the case of a dairy farmer in Shropshire. He will have invested money in buying all the specialised milking equipment he needs and may have modernised his milking parlour to house it. He has used his experience to improve the quality of his herd over many years and it is now very valuable. There is a very efficient collection service for the milk from a large dairy in the nearby town and he is able to sell off his unwanted male cattle in the market there. Most of his neighbours are dairy farmers and he would be unhappy to start a new type of farming and be different from them. If he did want to concentrate on cereals he would need to buy a lot of new equipment. Combine harvesters are very expensive. In any case, to use all this new equipment efficiently he would need a larger farm than he now has. Running a dairy farm would have to become unprofitable for him to change to something else.

Fig. 8.6. Annual rainfall of the West Midlands.

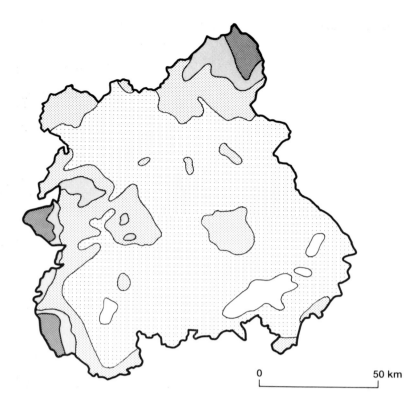

0   50 km

Copy out the passage on page 84, starting at 'He will have invested money. . .'. Underline all the reasons for not changing, and decide which of the factors 2 to 5 in fig. 8.4 each reason relates to.

This does not mean that farmers never change their types of farming. Table 29 gives you some data on how farming has changed in Warwickshire since 1950.

Table 29 *Changes in farming in Warwickshire since 1950.*

	1950	1960	1970	1980
Area of land used for:				
(i) wheat	24.4	23.0	24.9	41.2
(ii) barley	6.7	15.9	33.5	27.3
in thousand hectares				
The amount produced on each hectare of land growing:				
(i) wheat	2.4	3.4	4.2	5.3
(ii) barley	2.4	3.0	3.3	4.5
in tonnes				
Number of cattle reared in thousands	158	152	144	128

To make the changes clearer, draw three graphs: one for changes in area (using different coloured lines for wheat and barley); one for yield; and one for number of cattle.

Work out how much wheat and barley was actually produced.

What are the important changes that have taken place in Warwickshire?

You have probably decided that the trend in farming in Warwickshire has been to increase cereal production, especially barley. This has been made possible by growing fewer other crops, particularly grass. This means that cereals are now grown more often on the same land. At the same time the number of cattle reared has decreased, but not rapidly. To explain how and why this change has been possible we must refer to factors 6 to 8 on fig. 8.4. Since about 1960 the government has been encouraging farmers to increase cereal production, by raising the price that farmers get when they sell their cereals. This has continued since we joined the Common Market and has been so successful that Britain is now nearly self-sufficient in cereals. If you look at fig. 8.7 you can see some of the effects this change has had on the landscape. This farm is next door to the one in fig. 8.1 but it looks different in several ways. All the land you can see has just grown cereals. All the hedges have been pulled out. This is so that combine harvesters and other machinery can work more efficiently and reduce the costs. But to keep the land fertile more fertilisers are used now than there used to be. The land is now too valuable as cereal land for grass to be grown and for animals to graze on it, so that there is **zero grazing**. The animals that are kept, mainly cattle, are fed indoors in the buildings to the left of the farmhouse. The cattle are fed on cereals and concentrated food pellets, which are stored in the silos behind the cattle sheds. The cattle can be fed directly from the silos with the minimum of labour.

It is important to remember that despite the differences between these two neighbouring farms they have very similar physical conditions. The contrasts between them are caused by the different ways in which the farmers have decided to use their land. One farmer has chosen to stick to traditional ways of running a mixed farm. The other has chosen to adopt new methods. This does not mean that the farmer who chooses new methods is a better farmer.

zero grazing

This method of rearing animals is sometimes called zero grazing because they spend all their life inside animal sheds and are not allowed out to graze. Using this method, cattle reach slaughtering weight more quickly or produce more milk because they do not waste energy walking around, and save energy because they are sheltered from the weather.

This is an example of intensive farming. The aim of intensive farming is to produce large quantities of food from a small area of land using as little labour as possible.

Fig. 8.7. A cereal farming landscape near Stratford upon Avon, Warwickshire.

From the description of the farm in fig. 8.7, make a list of the differences which involve

(i) a reduction in production costs,
(ii) an increase in production costs,
(iii) an increase in income because of higher market prices which have resulted from price support policies.

Think about what would happen if the price of cereals fell.

The Vale of Evesham

How does a farming tradition grow and an area develop a specialised type of farming? If you look back at fig. 8.3 you will see that Hereford and Worcester has more land devoted to fruit and vegetable growing than any other county in the West Midlands. One area where this type of farming is concentrated is the Vale of Evesham. On the photograph of Evesham (fig. 7.2) all the area beyond the town is used for fruit and vegetables. The development of this type of farming is a good illustration of the idea of cumulative causation (see p. 33).

Before the middle of the nineteenth century, this area was an important cereal growing area. However, the growth of the industrial towns of the Midlands and the London area created a demand for fruit and vegetables. The coming of the railways meant it was possible for even remote rural areas to provide them quickly and cheaply. The Vale of Evesham was one of the areas that changed its farming to meet this new market. The factors which encouraged this change are:

(a) The presence of grade 1 and 2 farmland along the terraces of the River Avon (fig. 8.3). This deep, fertile soil gave the growers the opportunity to grow a wide range of crops.

(b) The Evesham area has an earlier spring than anywhere else in the West Midlands and this gives the growers the chance to sell their produce earlier at higher prices. It also gives a longer growing season and means that it is possible to grow several crops on one plot of land.

(c) The farming is intensive and the farms are usually small; 80% of them are less than 8 hectares. Because the plots are so small they are now difficult to convert to other types of farming.

(d) Most of the farmers are tenants on plots owned by the County or District Councils but they are encouraged to improve their land by the 'Evesham Custom'. If they leave their smallholding the Custom allows them to get compensation from the new tenant for all the tree crops, the buildings (especially glasshouses) and the value of manure. New tenants are only willing to pay out this compensation if they are going to carry on with the same type of farming.

(e) The area has developed specialised services to support market gardening. In Evesham, for example, there are cold storage facilities, specialised transport firms and a farmers' co-operative. The area also has specialised training at Pershore College of Horticulture and research at Evesham and at the National Vegetable Research Station at Wellesbourne.

All these factors continue to encourage specialisation. We have already seen the dangers of specialisation in industry in chapter 5.

What problems does the area suffer as a result of cheap imports of apples from France and tomatoes from the Netherlands? Is it easy to change the system of farming? Use fig. 8.4 to help you decide.

Rural areas set up as a result of
government policy, planned to surround
the conurbations and some of the large
towns in the UK. The first one was set
up around London as a result of the
1947 Town and Country Planning Act.
The government began to encourage
the designation of Green Belts around
other urban areas in 1955. This
resulted in the identification of Green
Belts around the main built-up areas of
Birmingham, the Black Country,
Coventry, Stoke-on-Trent and
Newcastle under Lyme.
The aims of Green Belts are:
(i) to prevent continued outward
   growth of cities,
(ii) to preserve the rural character
   within the Green Belt,
(iii) to provide areas of rural recreation
   near to large cities.

The urban impact on the countryside

Although most of the land in the countryside is used for farming it is
also affected by the activities of people who live and work in towns.
These activities bring pressures on the countryside which are causing it
to change (see fig. 8.8). This urban impact can be recognised in three
sorts of change:
(a) the expansion of towns into the countryside immediately around
   them;
(b) people moving from the towns to live in villages;
(c) people from the towns using the countryside for recreation and
   leisure.
The land most under pressure is in the areas immediately around the
large urban areas in the West Midlands: the Birmingham–Black Country
conurbation and Stoke-on-Trent/Newcastle under Lyme. In an attempt
to control the effects of these towns an area around them has been set
aside as a **Green Belt**. In it the building of houses and factories is
severely restricted and every effort is made to preserve the open
character of the countryside. You can think of the countryside in general
and Green Belts in particular as areas where the interests of the
townspeople may be in conflict with the interests of the country people.

Fig. 8.8. Urban pressures on the countryside.

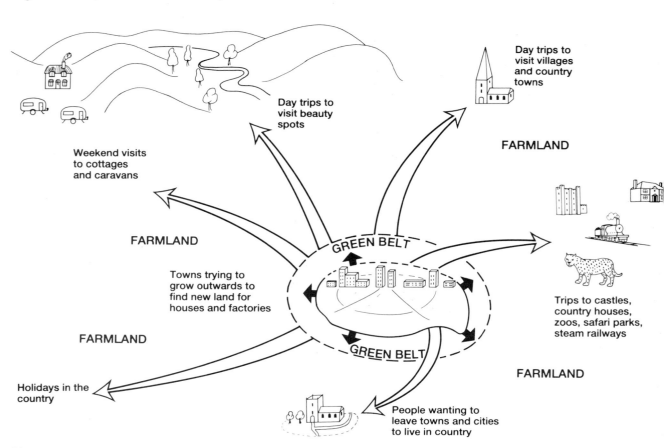

Urban expansion

As a town or city grows, its Council will probably think the surrounding countryside has the following attractions:

(a) There is space available for suburbs and overspill estates.

(b) There is space available for new industrial areas away from overcrowded Inner City locations.

(c) It is a good location for services which they would prefer not to have in the town itself because they may be dirty or unpleasant, for example sewage works, rubbish tips and electric power stations.

(d) It is a good location for services that would take up too much expensive space in the town, such as golf courses, large sports fields and airports.

These types of land use that need a lot of space or are dirty are often found on the **urban fringe**. The services found there are just near enough to be within easy reach of the town but not too near to be a nuisance. The urban fringe is the area where the Green Belt is most at risk. In the West Midlands the part of the Green Belt where these risks are at their greatest lies between Birmingham and Coventry. The open space between them is only 8 km wide at its narrowest point. If the Green Belt was not there to prevent it, the two cities could have grown outwards until they joined to form a new conurbation.

ban fringe

e narrow zone of land where the wn and country meet. It is the area here there is the greatest conflict tween the interests of town dwellers d country dwellers.

g. 8.9. The Green Belt between rmingham and Coventry.

ey

▦	Built-up areas of Birmingham and Coventry
▦	Birmingham overspill estates (60,000 population) K = Kingshurst C = Chelmsley Wood built in the late 1960s and early 1970s
– –	Birmingham boundary
▨	Villages
●—	Railway stations
P	Golf course
P	Packington Park (important angling/ fishing site)
▲	Shustoke Reservoir (sailing)
S	Sports grounds
▨	Birmingham Airport extended in the early 1980s
NEC	National Exhibition Centre built in the 1970s
◣	Industrial estate
⛏	Sand and gravel quarry
▲	Coal mine
○ ○	Sewage works
▯	Electric power station
	Open countryside

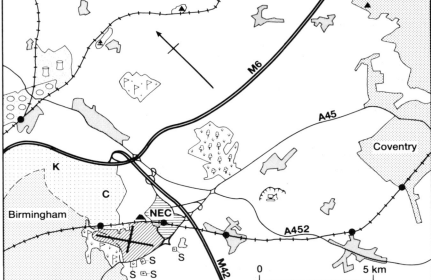

Fig. 8.10. The National Exhibition Centre. (The photograph was taken just east of the M42, looking towards Birmingham Airport.)

Use the map (fig. 8.9) to identify the pressures on and changes taking place in the Green Belt:
1. Identify on the map typical urban fringe land uses.
2. What evidence is there on the map to suggest that open countryside is being lost to   (i) urban expansion
            (ii) village growth
            (iii) recreation?
   In what other ways is land being lost?
3. The National Exhibition Centre (NEC) was built on the edge of Birmingham, and like so many other urban fringe activities it uses a lot of space (fig. 8.10). In what ways is the space used on the NEC site?
4. Can you suggest why the decision was taken to allow so much Green Belt land to be used for the NEC? What benefits do you think it brings to the area?

The changing village

In chapter 4 we looked at how people were moving out of the towns and were buying new houses in surrounding areas. We also saw that most of the rural areas were gaining population. But how is the countryside able to cope with this influx of people? If too many people move into the villages looking for a quiet country life, will they destroy the peaceful surroundings they are looking for? Should the newcomers be allowed to move to any village they choose and risk all the villages being spoiled by rapid growth?

All the rural counties of the West Midlands have tried to regulate the growth of villages by selecting certain villages to absorb most of the immigrants and thus protect the others. The villages selected for growth are called 'key settlements' or 'key villages'. Almost all new housing, services and any small industry have to be located in them. You might think this is hard luck on the villages that are chosen! How would you feel about the policy if you were an old inhabitant of one of the key villages or you wanted to move out of Birmingham and wanted to live in a small village? Not surprisingly, not everyone thinks that the key settlement policy is a good way of planning in rural areas. Critics argue that in the expanding villages the old village is overwhelmed as it becomes surrounded by new housing estates and the atmosphere of the village is lost. Sometimes 'us and them' attitudes may develop between the old and the new villagers. In villages where growth is prevented decay may set in as schools, churches and shops close and bus services are cut. As there are no jobs in the village, people have to commute to work.

The information in fig. 8.11 was collected on a field visit to six villages in Warwickshire.

Can you identify which one is the 'key settlement'?
What do you think are the advantages and disadvantages of living in Hampton Lucy, Wasperton and Wellesbourne?

Fig. 8.11. Field Survey Record: village services.

Field Survey Record: Village services

Location WARWICKSHIRE   Date 14th AUGUST 1982

Services	Wasperton	Charlecote	Hampton Lucy	Loxley	Wellesbourne	Newbold Pacey
Church	√	√	√	√	√√	√
Post box and Phone box	√	√	√	√	√√ +	√
Post Office	√				√	
Public house/Hotel		√	√	√	√√√	
Primary school			√	√	√	
Village hall/Club		√			√√√ √	
Food shops			√		√√√√ √√√√	
Other shops					√√√√ √√√√ √√	
Services					√√√√ √√√√ √√	
Medical services					√√√ √√√	
Recreation ground		√			√	
Others not above					√ Council Eng. + Road Depot.	
New houses						
Private estate			√√		√√√√√	
Council estate			√		√	
Renovation/Infilling	√	√	√	√	√	
Industry						
Record details					√ See below *	

*Wellesbourne Airfield Industrial Estate
(i) Pianoforte Supplies Plastics   (iv) Irrigation Services
(ii) Henleys Cars   (v) Avon Sprays — Agricultural ?
(iii) A storage/distribution firm   (vi) 3 factories with names but no product given

Recreation in the countryside

If you look back at fig. 8.8 you will see that there are many ways in which people want to use the countryside for pleasure. The most beautiful areas are set aside as **National Parks** and **Areas of Outstanding Natural Beauty (AONB)**. These are found in the hilly and mountainous areas on the edges of the West Midlands and are a relatively long way from most of the towns but they can all be reached on day trips. Other attractive areas are in the Green Belts. These are not so beautiful but have the advantage of being close to towns. Parts of them can be reached by public transport and so are accessible to many more people. Although many people still want to go into the country and 'please themselves' about what they do, others are attracted to particular places by the facilities provided there. Providing these facilities has led to the growth of a countryside leisure and recreation industry which provides work for people living in the country and brings money into the country areas. The main areas of tourist activity are shown in fig. 8.12.

A good example of a recreation area in the Green Belt but on the very edge of the built-up area is Sutton Park. It is a remnant of a medieval forest which was used for hunting. It now has woodland, heath, marsh and grassland. During the eighteenth century some of the valleys were dammed to make mill ponds for small water-powered industries. These pools are now used for fishing and boating, and are the homes for many water fowl and other wild life. The photographs in fig. 8.13 show the two faces of Sutton Park as a recreation area. About a million visitors use the park each year. The activities they take part in include the following:

Areas of Outstanding Natural Beauty (AONB)
Areas which have attractive scenery where the natural beauty is worth conserving for both local and national interests. Recreational use is developed only as far as it is consistent with the conservation of the landscape.

National Parks
Created in England and Wales after the passing of an Act of Parliament in 1949 (The National Parks and Access to the Countryside Act). Parks have been set up in the following places:
1951 Peak District; Lake District; Snowdonia; Dartmoor
1952 Pembrokeshire Coast; North York Moors
1954 Yorkshire Dales; Exmoor
1956 Northumberland
1957 Brecon Beacons.
They are large areas of beautiful and relatively wild countryside which are to be used for the nation's benefit.

Fig. 8.12. Recreation in the West Midlands:
(a) The use of the countryside for leisure.

(b) Valued landscapes.

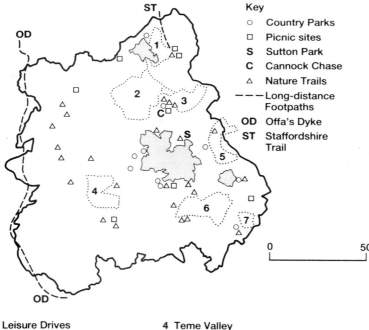

Key
○ Country Parks
□ Picnic sites
S Sutton Park
C Cannock Chase
△ Nature Trails
--- Long-distance Footpaths
OD Offa's Dyke
ST Staffordshire Trail

0   50 km

||||| Green Belt
☐ Built-up area
Peak District National Park
Areas of Outstanding Natural Beauty (AONB)

Leisure Drives
1 Potteries and Moorlands
2 Staffordshire Parklands
3 Vale of Trent
4 Teme Valley
5 North Warwickshire
6 Historic Warwickshire
7 Warwickshire Cotswolds

walking	bird watching	studying wild plants
photography	painting and	picnicking
swimming	sketching	sailing
golf	boating	sunbathing
flying kites	cycling	paddling in children's
having rides on	flying model	pool
children's swings	aeroplanes	
and roundabouts		

Fig. 8.13. Recreational land uses in Sutton Park.

(a)

(b)

1. Which of these activities will lead to people crowding together as they are in fig. 8.13(a)?
2. Which of the activities need plenty of open space?
3. Which activities depend on the park being an area of open countryside? Which depend on special facilities being provided?
4. What problems might arise with so many people using the park?

You should see from your answers to these questions how Sutton Park illustrates one of the problems of using country areas for recreation. The problem, which is another example of cumulative causation, works out as follows:

(a) People are attracted to an area because it is in the country. It is attractive because of the open space and the peace and quiet.

(b) Because a lot of people use the area, special facilities are provided. These may be just public lavatories and cafés to start with, but in time other things may be built.

(c) Even more people begin to use the area and it will begin to lose its attractions as an area of open country.

You might like to discuss in class some of the issues this problem raises. For example:

1. Should people be encouraged to use the countryside for recreation if this involves spoiling some areas?
2. Should people from the towns be kept out of some areas in the country?
3. Should some parts of the countryside be used especially for recreation? If so, should they be near to towns or should they be a long way from them, so that fewer people use them?

Whatever your opinions are about this, one thing is clear. Although farming is still the most typical activity in rural areas, the countryside of the West Midlands will continue to change as more people want to live and work there and as more people use it for their leisure activities.

9 The West Midlands into the future

Much of this book has been about the forces or processes which are bringing about change in the West Midlands. Long after you leave school, when you are no longer studying geography, perhaps what you have learnt here will help you to make sense of the changes you see around you. These changes will certainly affect your lives and are issues that are likely to be in the news.

If current trends in employment continue these might be the changes which result:

Deindustrialisation: fewer people will work in manufacturing industry, and this will affect the metal trade more than others. More people are likely to find jobs in the service industries. This may mean that women will find it easier to get jobs than men.

Industrial evolution: traditional industries will develop new products. For example, ARG will develop new cars, GEC will become more involved with satellite communication systems, and so on. But new technologies may mean that this will generate fewer jobs.

Industrial diversification: new industries will develop to help fill gaps left by the closure of traditional industries. One recent example is the growth of the clothing trade, mainly making anoraks and casual wear. This has relied heavily on money from within the Asian community and employs mainly Asian women, who were previously unemployed.

High technology industries: these involve the industrial application of new scientific discoveries, for example in computing and microbiology. Such industries are often sited in science parks, like those at Aston and Warwick Universities, but they will become more widespread.

The quality of the housing you live in is also going to be an issue. Many of the region's oldest houses have already been replaced. However, between 25% and 35% of houses in the West Midlands were built between 1919 and 1939. During your lifetime they will need replacing or modernising. Even more of a problem are the houses and flats (especially the high-rise blocks) built in the last 25 years which are already in poor repair. In the next 20 years a lot of money will have to be spent on housing, and the urban landscape will undergo big changes.

Any geographical change involves people arguing over different ways in which the land may be used. If we

(a) want to prevent Inner Cities becoming derelict,

(b) want new land for industry and housing,

(c) continue to move out of towns to live in rural areas,

(d) want to continue exploiting mineral resources,

(e) have shorter working weeks and more time for recreation,

(f) expect our farmers to produce more and cheaper food,

(g) have more people owning cars in future and need more roads

and so on, then the future of your environment will continue to be an important issue. Perhaps this book has helped you to develop some ideas of the ways in which you might want to influence those changes.

Index

Page numbers in italics refer to tables or illustrations.